FROM PETIPA TO BALANCHINE

FROM PETIPA TO BALANCHINE

CLASSICAL REVIVAL AND THE MODERNIZATION OF BALLET

Tim Scholl

London and New York

First published 1994
by Routledge
11 New Fetter Lane, London EC4P 4EE

Simultaneously published in the USA and Canada
by Routledge
29 West 35th Street, New York, NY 10001

Typeset in Perpetua by
Florencetype Ltd, Kewstoke, Avon

Printed and bound in Great Britain by
Biddles Ltd, Guildford and Kings Lynn

British Library Cataloguing Publication Data

A catalogue record for this book is available from the British Library

Library of Congress Cataloging in Publication Data

Scholl, Tim
From Petipa to Balanchine: classical revival and the modernization of ballet / Tim Scholl.
p. cm.
Includes bibliographical references (p.) and index.
1. Ballet — History — 19th century. 2. Ballet — History — 20th century. 3. Ballet —
Russia (Federation) — History — 19th century. 4. Ballet — Russia (Federation) —
History — 20th century. 5. Petipa, Marius, 1822–1910. 6. Balanchine, George. I. Title.
GV1787.S298 1993
792.8 – dc20   93–2102

ISBN 0–415–09222–1

CONTENTS

ILLUSTRATIONS

PREFACE

The modernization of Russian ballet — the transformation of an insular, court-sponsored elite entertainment to a commercially viable art form with a world-wide popular following — dates roughly from the reform movement begun in Russia's imperial theaters in the 1880s to the demise of the Diaghilev ballet in the late 1920s, when a number of "Russian" ballet troupes billed themselves as heirs to the imperial ballet legacy. Since then, Diaghilev's famous company, the Ballets Russes, has come to represent the flagship of ballet modernity. Writers on the period celebrate the company's collaborations with leading Russian and European composers and visual artists and laud the anti-establishment ethos of its iconoclastic choreographic experiments. This work takes a different view. Although the Diaghilev experiment clearly breathed new life into an increasingly moribund art form, the Ballets Russes left a scant legacy. By the end of the Diaghilev period, only a return to the classical dance's academy could revitalize the art.

This work examines the Russian ballet's classical revival — an anomalous feature of Russian arts and letters (especially of St Petersburg) in the first decades of the twentieth century, when turn-of-the-century Russian artists looked increasingly to the art of the past to invigorate and reorder their work. I use the term "retrospectivism" to describe an important first step in this process: the engagement with past art that typically results in borrowing or imitation. The artists discussed in this study looked to examples of past art they considered models; the resulting revival is rightly considered "classical." In early twentieth-century Russia, that term indicated an esteem for artistic ideals, regardless of period or place of origin.

I trace the classical revival in twentieth-century Russian arts and letters from a retrospectivism identifiable in imperial ballet productions *c.* 1890–1900, most notably in the 1890 production of *Sleeping Beauty*. By the turn of the century, this retrospectivism took two main forms: a revival of eighteenth-century neoclassicism (itself a retrospectivist mode) that idealized the artistic culture of pre-revolutionary France (and increasingly, Russian art of the same era); and a vogue of hellenism (nascent in Western culture from the time of Winckelmann, but popularized in fin de siècle Russia by the writings of Nietzsche and later by the dances of Isadora Duncan) inspired by the art of classical antiquity. Both these revivals played important roles in the development of ballet modernism. By the second phase of the Russian modernist movement (*c.* 1910), the first began to subsume the second.

The written record of Russian ballet stretches back over one century. Yet reminiscences, memoirs, and picture books far outnumber objective, researched accounts of the dance's history. One writer's observations on the general state of dance books has special relevance for works on this most celebrated period in the history of Russian ballet: "Shake them out and you would accumulate one small mound of method, one alpine peak of gossip, and, running between, a meandering stream of metaphysics" (Pierpont 1990, 82).

Historians of Russian ballet typically divide that history into distinct nineteenth-/twentieth-century and Russian/Western segments. There is some justification for this: Petipa's last viable works for the imperial theaters were created in 1900; the landmark ballets of the twentieth century's "new" ballet were shown primarily in Western Europe; and until recently, Balanchine's ballets were rarely seen in Russia. This study views the modern history of the Russian ballet as a continuous (though dislocated) tradition. Petipa's later works showed the way to much of the innovation of the future, and the choreography and pedagogy of Balanchine (though carried on primarily in the United States) represent the most important creative response to the legacy of Petipa's nineteenth-century ballet academy – and the most significant twentieth-century development of "Russian" ballet traditions.

This "academy" is the syllabus of the *danse d'école* – the vocabulary of classical dance. The work discusses the formation of a distinctly Russian school of classical dance late in the nineteenth century, its disintegration and reformulation in the twentieth. It also proposes a new view of the Russian nineteenth-century ballet academy: one whose grammar of structure and staging becomes as important as the dance steps themselves.

This work was not conceived as a comprehensive history of the period. Rather, it examines several landmark works that shape the course of modern ballet history. Marius Petipa and George Balanchine are the work's central figures. Although the first was French and the second worked primarily in the United States, these ballet masters were most responsible for the formation of the dominant ballet academies of their centuries, and both these academies are rightly called "Russian." Petipa was at the helm of the imperial ballet at the time its style first distinguished it from that of European companies; Balanchine's pedagogy and choreography engaged and furthered that tradition. (Some readers will expect to find choreographers such as Fyodor Lopukhov and Bronislava Nijinska discussed here. Although both choreographers are lately termed "neoclassicists," neither left a body of work that appreciably altered the development of the twentieth-century academy. Nijinska, for example, declared her allegiance to the classical school, but her choreography never realized the potential suggested by *Les Noces*.)

The ballets discussed here document the development of the Russian ballet's classical revival, from Petipa's *Sleeping Beauty* to Balanchine's *Apollo* and *Jewels*. These works reveal a gradual shift from a retrospectivism that venerates the traditions of the French court ballet to a reassessment of the inherent classicism of the *danse d'école*. In the ballet, as in other Russian art forms, this "classical" legacy increasingly included Russia's own (eighteenth- and nineteenth-century) contributions to the art form and incorporated these recent bequests into its twentieth-century definition of dance classicism.

Russian ballet was at the forefront of Russian artistic culture in the first decades of this century and a vital point of contact among the Russian arts in the modernist period (*c.* 1890–1930). Diaghilev's "formula" of ballet production represented an attempt to synthesize dance, music, and the visual arts into a nonverbal *Gesamtkunstwerk*, the idealized fusion of the arts Wagner imagined. Later, Balanchine would reject the imposition of visual art and narrative in the ballet. His preoccupation with music and space marked a return to a more basic definition of dance: movement in space and time. This reappraisal of the art form's inherent properties reflected typically modernist concerns, as the modern ballet's dominant aesthetic evolved from synaesthesia to minimalist purity.

Balanchine's fascination with three-dimensional stage space and the workings of the dancing body (and his rejection of Diaghilev's syncretistic "formula") suggests links to a later, "Petersburg" phase of Russian modernism, characterized by its admiration for architecture's fusion of form and function and its esteem for the art of the past. Like his contemporaries, the "acmeist" poets, Balanchine appealed to form as a means of exploiting the inherent qualities of their materials.

Some of the works discussed in this study have disappeared completely, others have been reconstructed. Some have survived in the ballet repertory much as originally produced, others have had their choreography altered over the years by performers and ballet masters. Some have been notated in systems legible to specialists, others were preserved in notation systems now forgotten and virtually indecipherable. A fortunate few of the ballets were filmed under the choreographer's supervision and can be viewed today in these "authentic" versions.

This highly irregular situation limits considerably the degree to which the ballets themselves can serve as primary materials for this study. Only the more recent, authentically preserved works can be analyzed in detail; the earlier, lost works cannot speak for themselves. In the majority of cases, where the extant choreography cannot be considered genuine, secondary sources are employed to bring the works to life. Newspaper reviews, photographs, letters, journal entries, eyewitness accounts, and performers' memoirs prove invaluable in attempting to discuss both surviving and lost works.

I have attempted to use the most standard titles of the Russian ballets discussed here, and accurate transliterations of Russian personal names. I use the original French titles for ballets that premièred in the Russian court theater and for the works given by Diaghilev's company in Europe. Unless otherwise noted, all translations are my own.

ACKNOWLEDGMENTS

I owe the first and largest debt of gratitude to Robert Jackson, Katerina Clark and Elizabeth Allen, who encouraged this study and read the work in its first version. Selma-Jeanne Cohen, Don Daniels, and Claudia Roth Pierpont also read portions of the work and offered valuable suggestions. I am grateful for the assistance provided by the librarians and archivists at Mount Holyoke College, Yale University, the Dance Collection of the New York Public Library, the library of the Paris Opera, and Ballet Society. Mount Holyoke College supported archival research in Paris.

Special thanks to Costas (whose photographs illustrate the text), David Gray and the press office of the New York City Ballet, Elizabeth Suritz and Oleg Petrov in Russia, colleagues in the Russian and dance departments at Mount Holyoke College, Rusty Barrett, Luc Beaudoin, Otto Bohlmann, Svetlana Evdokimova, Katherine Lahti, Dan St Laurent, Jane Sharp, Otis Stuart, Oleg Tarabuzan, and Tony Williams.

1

RUSSIAN BALLET IN THE LATE NINETEENTH CENTURY

IN *Our Ballet*, the first history of ballet in Russia, Aleksandr Pleshcheev traces the origins of Russian ballet to 1673, when, following a recitation of some German couplets, a ballet on the theme of Orpheus was presented to the court of Tsar Aleksei Mikhailovich: "the pas de trois of Orpheus and two pyramids was performed, and then Orpheus and the other participants – brilliantly dressed – executed several foreign national dances. The ballet performance greatly pleased Aleksei Mikhailovich" (Pleshcheev 1896, 29). The Orpheus ballet and the play *Artakserksovo deistvo* (a biblical drama based on the book of Esther presented in Aleksei Mikhailovich's court one year earlier) mark the beginning of imperial patronage of Russian theater and dance, a constant that enabled the ballet to survive in Russia long after its viability as an art form in Western Europe had ceased.

Like popular theater, dance existed in Russia long before the tsars began to support the arts, but these were folk traditions; the importation and adaptation of Western theatrical forms represented something very different. As visiting European troupes acquainted Russian audiences with the principal Western theatrical genres in the seventeenth and eighteenth centuries, Russian nobles began to train and maintain their own companies of entertainers. The orchestra assembled for the performance of

1

Artakserksovo deistvo was composed of foreigners and the household serfs of the tsar's favorite noble (ibid., 28).

The divergence from local amateur theatrical traditions was palpable: although the theatrical presentations of the *skomorokhi* (entertainers who acted, sang, and danced) held a place in the calendar of the Orthodox church already in the eleventh century, stagings of Western school dramas in the middle of the seventeenth century aroused the ire of Archpriest Avvakum, who denounced them as "Romanisms" (Hoover 1985, 470).

As in the West, where ballet evolved slowly from theatricalized social dancing in Renaissance courts, social dancing paved the way for the acceptance of stage dancing in Russia. Balls and assemblies assumed a primary socializing function in the court of Peter I. A 1718 decree required nobles to give and attend assemblies and outlined the rights and responsibilities of hosts and guests. Peter not only attended these assemblies, he also danced in them: "the sovereign himself took part in the dances and taught others to dance" (Pleshcheev 1896, 30). An eyewitness attested to his skill as a dancer: "the tsar performed cabrioles that would have made the best European ballet master of the day proud" (ibid.).

The public dancing initiated at Peter I's behest continued in the reigns of Catherine I, Anna, and Elizabeth, and laid the groundwork for the establishment of Russia's court ballet. The first imperial ballet school was organized during Anna's reign, in 1738, by Jean-Baptiste Landé, a French ballet master who had come to St Petersburg four years earlier. In the 1740s Elizabeth employed three ballet masters simultaneously: Landé to stage tragic ballets, Rinaldi Fossano for comic works, and Thomas Lebrun for allegorical ballets (ibid., 36). Even so, the ballet's continued presence in Russia was not assured: Pleshcheev writes that during Peter III's short reign in 1762, no performances were given due to the mourning following the death of Elizabeth (ibid., 41).

Catherine II's interest in the theater and the steps she took to create a state theater monopoly virtually guaranteed the future of ballet in Russia. She established the imperial theater system in 1756, created the directorate of the imperial theaters ten years later, saw to the construction of St Petersburg's Bolshoi Theater in 1773, and founded the imperial theater school (which trained actors, singers, and dancers) in 1779. By the end of the century, the ballet and its school were part of a well-organized imperial theater bureaucracy, and the list of European ballet masters associated with the Russian imperial ballet in its formative years includes several of the most important choreographers of the pre-romantic era.

Charles-Louis Didelot (1767–1837) worked in Russia from 1801 to 1811 and settled there permanently in 1816. Under Didelot, the imperial school and its syllabus began to assume its modern form and the Russian ballet enjoyed its first period of celebrity (his dances and his dancers were immortalized in Pushkin's *Eugene Onegin*). The titles of the works he staged in Russia (*Apollo and Daphnis*, *Flore and Zephyre*, *Medea and Jason*, *Amour and Psyche*, *Acis and Galatea*, to name but a few) reveal an eighteenth-century propensity for anacreontic plots drawn from Greek mythology, yet Didelot's stagings of these works (which frequently used machinery to "fly" his ballerinas across the stage) anticipated the elaborate "grand" ballet staging that Marius Petipa developed in the last half of the nineteenth century. Unfortunately, our knowledge of Didelot's work is limited to secondary sources; like the greater share of ballets created before the age of film documentation, Didelot's œuvre is lost.

In the years following Didelot's retirement in 1831, Europe's most celebrated ballerinas toured Russia: Marie Taglioni (1837–1842), Lucille Grahn (1843), Fanny Elssler (1848–1851), Carlotta Grisi (1850–1853) and Fanny Cerrito (1855–56). These women danced in local productions of romantic ballet vehicles in Russia: staples of the new "international" repertory such as *La Sylphide* and *Giselle*.[1]

In the 1850s and 1860s, Russia's imperial ballet attracted three of the nineteenth century's most talented ballet masters to St Petersburg. Jules Perrot worked in Russia from 1848 until 1859. Arthur Saint-Léon succeeded him in 1859 and choreographed for the imperial theaters until 1869. Marius Petipa, whose ballets define late nineteenth-century Russian ballet style, was engaged as a dancer in the St Petersburg ballet in 1847. Although Perrot and Saint-Léon each choreographed a number of ballets in the West and in Russia, the questionable authorship of their surviving works (later restaged and revised by Petipa) precludes any definitive estimation of these choreographers' lasting contributions to the Russian repertory.

Marius Petipa (1818–1910) had served as a dancer, assistant ballet master, and, from 1862, ballet master of the imperial ballet from the time of his engagement until Saint-Léon's retirement in 1869. He also taught in the theater school. With Saint-Léon's departure, his leadership went unchallenged.[2] The ballets he created in the 1860s and 1870s represent a choreographic response to nineteenth-century grand opera. The Petipa ballet grew into a multi-act spectacle, elaborately staged and performed by a complex hierarchy of dancers.

3

Petipa staged approximately 75 ballets for the Russian imperial theaters and arranged dances for 36 opera productions.[3] But only six of the full-length ballets choreographed by Petipa are still performed. Three of these date from the last phase of Petipa's career: *Sleeping Beauty* (1890), *Swan Lake* (1895),[4] and *Raymonda* (1898). These ballets, to music of Pyotr Tchaikovsky and Aleksandr Glazunov, are Petipa's best-known works. Standards of the international repertory, they have come down to us in reasonably authentic versions. The ballets that survive from the first decades of Petipa's work in Russia – *Le Corsaire* (1863), *Don Quixote* (1869), and *La Bayadère* (1877) – have suffered infrequent, less faithful revivals.

The grand ballet

Le Corsaire, *Don Quixote*, and *La Bayadère* are each described as a "*bol'shoi balet*" in the Soviet catalogue of Petipa's works (Slonimsky 1971, 377–388).[5] A translation of the French *ballet à grand spectacle*, the term is used to describe ballets that resemble nineteenth-century grand operas in their length, the complexity of their narratives, and tendency toward visual spectacle. Because these works dominated the Petersburg stage from the 1860s through the 1890s, and because Russian ballet had no serious competitors in Europe by the 1870s, the Petipa "grand ballet" has come to represent the ballet style of the late nineteenth century.

That style has been berated in the post-Diaghilev era by dance writers who choose to see the history of dance as an evolutionary progression to the aesthetic of Diaghilev's Ballets Russes. In his *Complete Book of Ballets*, Cyril Beaumont devotes nearly half his introduction of the Petipa ballets to an indictment of nineteenth-century Russian ballet production and performance practices (1941, 385–387). His main objections center around the primacy of dance in these productions in which, admittedly, music, scenery, and costumes were of secondary importance.[6] Beaumont's account includes a quote from Tamara Karsavina, the star of Diaghilev's early European seasons:

> Petipa had a remarkable command of mass on the stage and sometimes the form taken by his *ballabiles* showed considerable imagination. But his productions were all founded on the same formula. An inevitable *divertissement* brought his ballets to an ever happy conclusion; while such of his heroes, for whom anything but a tragic end was an historical impossibility, found

themselves crowned in a final apotheosis. His ballets tended to be "*féeries.*" In his later years he made some attempts to modernise his art to accord more nearly with the present time, but he never felt at ease when making these efforts and they were unsuccessful. His ballets, which even now have not disappeared from the repertory of the Maryinsky Theatre, were crowded with marches and processions which often interrupted, without any kind of logical excuse, long, continuous scenes of pantomime and beautifully composed dances.

(1941, 384–385)

Karsavina's remarks, written in 1912, at the height of her involvement with the Diaghilev company, echo Beaumont's objections to the Petipa ballet and repeat the historical inaccuracies he perpetuated. Beaumont privileges the so-called Diaghilev formula, in which music, design, and dancing are combined into a brief, wordless approximation of the Wagnerian *Gesamtkunstwerk* (the "total art work" Wagner hoped to achieve in the successful synthesis of the individual elements of an opera production). In fact, the shorter, one-act form made famous by the Ballets Russes had been used by Petipa throughout his career, especially in works for the court. Karsavina's reappraisal of Petipa in her 1930 autobiography redresses earlier biases and suggests the extent to which Petipa's works had begun to be appreciated in the West by that time:

In the history of our ballet [Petipa] will stand a providential figure of titanic strength. His genius was unquestioned during his lifetime, but the wealth of his inheritance could only have been appreciated retrospectively in connection with the new movement. The force of Petipa's creations reached out far beyond his lifetime and is not yet entirely spent.

(1981, 198)

The romantic ballet prototype

Many of Petipa's early works for the imperial stages were restagings of ballets originally produced in Paris from the 1830s to the 1850s, the height of ballet romanticism,[7] and Petipa's later, original works reveal thematic and structural debts to them. The basic themes, plot structure, and imagery of the ballets of the romantic period served as models for the ballets of the nineteenth century until the premise of narrative ballet was finally abandoned in the twentieth century.

Giselle (1841), the most durable and frequently staged ballet of the

French romantic repertory, furnishes the best example.[8] Like other heroines of the nineteenth-century lyric stage, Giselle selflessly "redeems" her unfaithful lover from beyond the grave. Martyred heroines were something of a commonplace of nineteenth-century opera, literature, and art,[9] but the opera and ballet theaters, using the relatively new technology of gas lighting and old standbys like tulle and muslin, were particularly adept at bringing these morbid themes to life. The ballet of dead nuns in Meyerbeer's 1831 opera, *Robert le Diable*, brought romantic themes and pseudo-gothic imagery to the lyric stage, inaugurating the brief but influential era of ballet romanticism.

The success of romantic ballets like *Giselle* and *La Sylphide* ensured their imitation; the martyred sylphs of the 1830s and 1840s are replicated endlessly in Petipa's ballets. Aspichia, the heroine of Petipa's first full-scale original work for the Maryinsky, *Daughter of the Pharaoh* (1862), drowns herself in the Nile rather than marry against her wishes. Nikia, the eponymous bayadère, is bitten by a poisonous snake. Aurora, the sleeping princess, loses a century to sleep. But like Giselle and the Sylphide, all return as spirits to dance the ballet's subsequent act.

The prevalence of theatricalized female sacrifice in Petipa's works gave rise to a standardized plot structure. The typical Petipa work has a mad scene, a vision scene, and a scene of reconciliation in which the male protagonist and heroine are rejoined – with each scene slightly adapted to the new narrative exigencies. In *Sleeping Beauty*, for example, Aurora's madness is not literal, but the prick with the evil fairy's spindle satisfies a similar structural demand: it brings the realistic scene to its close and necessitates the fantastic scene that follows, in which Aurora appears as a vision during her hundred-year sleep. Likewise, Aspichia appears underwater after drowning in *Daughter of the Pharaoh*, and Nikia is next seen in *La Bayadère*'s Kingdom of the Shades.

In *Giselle*, the two lovers are reunited in a final pas de deux before the light of dawn signals his freedom and her return to the grave. In the Petipa ballet, this resolution expands to occupy an entire scene (*Daughter of the Pharaoh* and *Sleeping Beauty* end in wedding celebrations). Where reconciliation was impossible, the final scene offered resolution. In *Bayadère*, the dead Nikia cannot return to earth; instead, she causes a storm which collapses the palace, killing her philandering lover, her rival, and the remainder of the ballet's on-stage personnel.

Ultimately, the structure, rather than the themes of the romantic ballet proved most important for Petipa, as the literal or metaphoric death of the heroine became less significant than the narrative structure it determined. The fantastic scene of the romantic ballet, the *ballet blanc*, or "white act" divertissement for the female corps de ballet and soloists, became a standard feature of Petipa's full-length ballets, present even in comic works like *Don Quixote* (1869). In that ballet, the Don's dream of Dulcinea takes the form of a *ballet blanc* in which Dulcinea is joined by Kitri, the ballet's heroine, and a corps de ballet of dryads. When Petipa restaged *Le Corsaire* in 1868, he added a similar white scene to the work – this time, a *jardin animé*.

Expansion of this sort typified the Petipa ballet. Where the romantic ballet's structure was essentially dual, juxtaposing day and night, reality and fantasy, the grand ballet grew to an average of four acts with upwards of nine scenes. This was accomplished primarily by extending and complicating the narrative while retaining the basic structure of the romantic ballet: the *ballet blanc* for the female corps followed the first, narrative sequences; the final act took the form of a grand divertissement, with an assortment of national and/or character dances.

Staging the grand ballet

The structural expansion of Petipa's ballets found its analog in the increasingly elaborate productions these works received. *Daughter of the Pharaoh* (1862) was the first of Petipa's grand ballets, and remained the most ambitious, with three acts and nine scenes, including an epilog and prolog.[10] The action takes place in ancient Egypt. After the ballet's hero, the English Egyptologist Lord Wilson, smokes opium, he dreams that he and his servant (John Bull) have entered the world of the mummified Egyptians they have discovered. Lord Wilson wishes to marry the Pharaoh's daughter, Aspichia, who is also claimed by the King of Nubia. When forcibly taken by the King, Aspichia jumps to her death in the Nile. The King of the Nile eventually returns Aspichia to the earth, where she marries Wilson in the ballet's final act.

The ballet's most spectacular dance sequence takes place under the Nile, where dancers representing the rivers Guadalquivir, Thames, Rhine, Congo, Tiber, and Neva (and the Moscow river in that city's production), together with lesser soloists representing their respective tributaries and streams, dance in honor of Aspichia. This fantastic scene is analogous to the romantic *ballet blanc*: its extended divertissement follows the opening narrative scenes, furnishing another level of fantasy in a work already framed by a dream sequence.[11]

The entire production could only be described as grandiose. Two apotheosis scenes precede the ballet's final one. The first of these occurs in the prolog, when the mummified Aspichia comes to life as a ray of light falls upon her. The second closes the underwater scene as a jet of water from an on-stage fountain appears to raise Aspichia back to earth. The final apotheosis shows Lord Wilson still asleep while Egyptians celebrate the wedding; Osiris, Isis and various other ancient Egyptian deities are visible in the stage's "heavens" (Krasovskaya 1963, 234–235; Beaumont 1941, 391–400).

The choreography and staging Petipa devised for the ballet were similarly ostentatious. The ballet's *grand ballabile des cariatides animées* featured 36 dancers with baskets of flowers on their heads containing children who suddenly appeared in the dance's final pose. Tamara Karsavina remembers an even larger crowd in the ballet's hunt scene:

> The ballerinas, soloists and the corps de ballet number nearly forty persons appearing at one time on the stage. Later the numerous participants in the cortège of the Pharaoh were added to that number. The cortège appeared at the top of a high platform towards the rear of the stage and was gradually lowered. The platform had three levels, offering a winding descent from the mountain (poetic license, I suppose, or were there mountains in Egypt?). This in itself made for an effective entrance.
>
> The stage in question was constructed thusly: One group of the Pharaoh's servants, carrying stylized palm fronds, arranged themselves behind the dancing corps de ballet. Behind this screen supers in corresponding costumes carried in blocks and arranged them in pyramid configurations. In order to get up onto them, two groups of the corps went around the palm-carriers and one, in the middle, moved to the rear of the stage, to the back drop. At the right time, revealing the center, the palm-carriers, one after the other, gradually got down on their knees, lowering their frond and forming a frieze, framing the rising group. The process of ascending onto the blocks was hidden in this way, and there was no turmoil during the movement.
>
> (1971, 309–310)

Petipa's choreography for the grand ballet represents the culmination of the evolution of a particular type of theatrical dancing, designed to exploit the scenic potential of the proscenium stage. The ballet's emphasis of the human body's maximal legibility evolved as the Renaissance perspective stage was developed. As dance performances began to be viewed frontally, framed by a proscenium arch, ballet choreography shifted its focus from patterns described on a ballroom floor, legible from the sides of the performance space, to emphasize the body's vertical and horizontal assertions on the picture-frame stage. The basic positions of ballet – feet and arms rotated outward from the body with limbs extended – make the dancers' movements maximally visible to the audience. The erect body, the leaps and jumps into the air, and the poses and movements executed high on the toes represent the ballet's conquest of vertical space on the new stage.

The elaborate scenic configurations Petipa devised for his ballets represent the zenith of a type of staging that also owes its origins to the Renaissance, when paintings "in perspective" began to be used as stage backdrops. Design – both scenic and choreographic – for the perspective stage assumed a vanishing point and an ideal spectator, whose view of the stage would determine the visual design of the production. Against backdrops painted in perspective, dancers and supernumeraries were arranged to give a false perception of the stage's recession, making the stage appear much deeper than it was. Alexandra Danilova recalls her childhood appearances in this type of production in St Petersburg's Maryinsky Theater in the years immediately preceding the 1917 revolution:

> We children were used primarily to create false perspective. The stage was raked, and we stood all the way at the back, giving the illusion, as people got smaller in the distance, of a crowd much deeper than the stage.
>
> (1986, 33–34)[12]

Considerably less attention was lavished on the overall design of the productions. Vladimir Telyakovsky, Director of Imperial Theaters from 1910 to 1917, recalled that the theaters' artists specialized in particular genres. "Designers were divided according to their painting specialties: architectural, forest, marine, and other types of décor. These designers never did costume or prop design" (1965, 161–162).[13] Nor did they plan the ballets as visually integrated productions. Telyakovsky describes the nineteenth-century ballet production as an assemblage of parts:

> When a new production was staged, the décors of the acts, painted by various designers, were assembled, as well as the costumes and props, executed according to the designs of Ponomarev, Vsevolozhsky himself, and others. The manner of execution, the tones, and colors – all of this differed in each act, often they didn't suit each other at all, and it was impossible to gain a coherent impression from the entire production.
>
> (ibid., 162)

The relative unimportance of ballet scenery was demonstrated when imperial ballet productions moved from St Petersburg's Bolshoi Theater to the narrower stage of the Maryinsky Theater in 1885: the sets that no longer fitted were replaced with décor from "forgotten operas" (Skalkovsky 1899, 228). Nor were scenes authenticated in the manner of theater productions of later years. The ballerina Ekaterina Vazem recalls: "In those bygone days in the theater little attention was generally paid to ethnographic or historical accuracy. They were especially indifferent to this in the ballet, where more than anything else, they worried about the beauty and brilliance of the production" (1937, 133).

The costume design for ballet productions went largely uncredited. *Don Quixote* (1869) had three set designers, with no credit for costume design; *La Bayadère* (1877) had five designers for seven scenes, again without credit for the costumes. Stage properties were purchased and warehoused, to be used as needed. Karl Valts, designer and machinist for the Bolshoi Theater in Moscow and a contemporary of Petipa, recalls a large purchase of properties made by the head of the Bolshoi Theater in Moscow in 1862:

> Lvov, in the interest of raising the public's interest in decorative art, found a way to order several décors of Professor Groppius in Berlin and sent for a large quantity of new props from Paris. The Lvov helmets, shields, swords, crowns and assorted decorations are still in use in the Bolshoi Theater.
>
> (1928, 35–36)

The catalog of the Russian exhibit at the International Musical and Theatrical Exhibition held in Vienna in 1892 lists a great many stage properties, described much like museum pieces ("shield, German, ninth century; dagger, Caucasian, decorated with stones") but no indication of their uses in actual productions or their designers (*Ezhegodnik imperatorskikh teatrov* 1890–1891, Supplement).

The painted backdrop functioned as the basic element of the ballet's stage design, but the designers worked closely with the theater's machinists to produce special effects. In Moscow, Karl Valts held both titles. In his introduction to Valts' memoirs, I. Sollertinsky suggests the range of the nineteenth-century stage designer's craft:

> The old type of designer was a wise pyrotechnician . . . who still hadn't lost the secret of the theatrical immolation of fire works or the inexpensive amateur means of creating grand fires and figurative fireworks on the stage. . . . Together with him goes the whole fireworks and pyrotechnic culture of the old theater.
>
> (Valts 1928, 6–7)

10

Clearly, Russian ballet in the late nineteenth century was an "art of spectacle," [*zrelishchnoe iskusstvo*] whose static, pictorial groupings and special effects could command as much attention as the actual dancing. The predominance of visual effects in these productions relegated music to a secondary position. Petipa's main musical collaborators were ballet composers in the imperial theaters' employ, hired to create on demand.[14] Skilled in the art of *pastiche*, they could refashion an existing work to meet new choreographic exigencies, or even write music to suit pre-existing choreography. Roland Wiley describes this situation in *Tchaikovsky's Ballets*:

> In Tchaikovsky's time the first law of ballet was the ballet master's precedence: other collaborators worked to his order, and he enjoyed complete power of veto over them. He was able to do this because he made the dances and the dances were the most unpredictable element in ballet, unwritten, largely irretrievable if forgotten, and in most cases thoroughly understood only by him. "Both the composer and the librettist in ballet should be subordinate to the ballet master," explains Alexander Pleshcheyev; "pride should submit to experience."
>
> (1985, 1)

As Karsavina's description of the hunt scene in *Daughter of the Pharaoh* suggests, the grand ballet frequently found its strength in numbers. The Petersburg ballet numbered 143 women and 69 men during the 1890–1891 season. In addition, the children of the theater school regularly took part in ballet productions, as did regiments of soldiers stationed around St Petersburg. These supernumeraries might be used in the type of crowd scenes Danilova describes, or to run under the on-stage tarpaulins, providing the waves for *Corsaire*'s shipwreck scene. The increase in on-stage personnel gave rise to an elaborate hierarchy of dancers in the Petipa ballet, as the stage began to mirror the social stratification of its audience. The ballerina became the stage's queen, supported by a consort and surrounded by minions of soloists, demi-soloists and corps de ballet dancers. This hierarchy affected the structure of the dances within the acts. The pas de deux, originally a danced duet, evolved into a "grand" pas that included soloists and a corps de ballet. Petipa's 1881 restaging of *Paquita* included a newly choreographed grand pas for the ballerina and her cavalier, soloists, and demi-soloists.

Eventually, the plethora of solo *pas* and *ballabiles* began to undermine the narrative structure of Petipa's danced dramas. The increasing prominence of solo variations (especially those for the female dancers) in Petipa's works reached its apogee in *Raymonda* (1898), Petipa's penultimate full-length ballet. In that work, the heroine has two female friends whose solo variations precede her own. The result is a work best viewed as a series of solos, as the quantity and quality of the dancing overwhelm the complex, incoherent plot.

Petipa and the Russian school

It is impossible to speak of the choreography of Petipa's ballets with absolute certainty as the greater share of it has passed from one generation of dancers to the next by memory alone. Although a few of Petipa's works were notated in the early years of this century, the "oral" tradition remained the predominant mode of teaching and learning dances until the relatively recent phenomenon of video.[15] It is possible to gauge the extent of Petipa's innovation by comparing his works to those of his contemporary, August Bournonville, active as a choreographer in Copenhagen's Royal Danish Ballet from 1830 to the 1870s. The differences between the two men's choreography and ballets are striking, even though the structures of their ballets and the dance techniques they developed are based on similar French romantic models. (Both had studied with Auguste Vestris in Paris.) The most obvious differences in the two men's ballets center around their choreography for women. Bournonville's pas de deux are frequently unison or "mirror" dances, in which the man and woman perform identical steps in complementary directions. Petipa's ballets are constructed around their ballerinas, so that even the premier dancer in the pas de deux is relegated to a supporting role, a consort but never a king.[16] In an article describing Russia's "new" ballet, E. A. Stark put forth a definition of the "old" Petipa ballet: "the old ballet was the ballerina" (1911, 110). An 1899–1900 list of ballets given in St Petersburg from 1828 confirms Stark's assessment. The pertinent information given for each production includes the ballet's title, its date, and its ballerina (*Ezhegodnik*, Supplement 3, 53–108).

The ballerina's new prominence in the late nineteenth century derived from the advances made in female point technique. In the early 1800s, when female dancers of the romantic period began to replace the noble male heroes that dominated the ballet stages in the previous century, dancing *sur les pointes* began as a novelty. Poses and simple steps on the tips of the toes conveyed a sense of lightness and ethereality in romantic works. The technique evolved in the next decades as padded, then stiffened and blocked ballet slippers permitted greater mobility.

12

As ballet shoes were adapted and the technique developed, dancing on point became less a means of expression than a technical feat, however. In the Petipa ballet, the ballerina's point technique became the focus of her solo variations, other aspects of the choreography were designed to maximize its effects: in a pas de deux, the partner's support enables the ballerina to balance on point in a variety of poses and execute otherwise impossible series of multiple turns; as her partner lifts and carries her across the stage, the ballerina poses as if gracefully leaping. By the twentieth century, point tricks like the thirty-two fouettés – a series of thirty-two turns performed on one leg on point while the other leg "whips" around the body – proved the measure of a ballerina's mettle, and the "steel toes" of Petipa's ballerinas had become objects of derision. Still, Petipa's female variations, designed to show the technical strengths of featured ballerinas to best advantage, represent the highest achievement of Petipa's solo choreography.

Petipa's solo variations show his mastery in organizing the vocabulary of the *danse d'école* into articulate, eloquent choreographic statements; his choreography for the female corps de ballet demonstrates his skill in deploying large on-stage ensembles in order to best exploit the spatial possibilities of the perspective stage. In the Kingdom of Shades scene of *Bayadère*, for example, members of the corps de ballet enter one by one from the back of the stage executing a very simple series of steps and poses, accompanied by a repetitive melodic line, until the entire stage is filled. The effect is that of an infinity of dancers, extending to the stage's vanishing point.[17] The corps of a Petipa ballet may form a barrier like the one that prevents Desiré from reaching Aurora in the vision scene of *Sleeping Beauty*, or a corridor leading him to her. The miracle of these scenes is the quick transformation of the ensemble from a decorative picture-frame for solo dances, to a palpable dramatic presence on the stage, and the rapidity with which Petipa's corps can transform an intimate space on the stage into one which seems to transcend the walls of the theater.

In her memoirs, Ekaterina Vazem consistently downplays Petipa's role in the formation of the Russian dance academy in the late nineteenth century – a view contradicted by the vast majority of writers on this subject – yet her recollections of the choreography of Petipa's predecessors undermine her own assertions. She considers Perrot a "ballet dramaturge," rather than a choreographer (1937, 53); and despite her high esteem for Saint-Léon's solo variations, she recalls that "the dancers danced on point very little" (ibid., 55). Vazem's personal preferences notwithstanding, it was Petipa who shaped the Russian dance academy, incorporating the best traditions of Europe's national ballet schools into an academy that offered a distinct profile in the late nineteenth century and assumed a dominant position among them in the twentieth.

Russian ballet in transition

Imperial patronage enabled the Russian ballet to prosper in the late nineteenth century, at a time when ballet in Western Europe was in decline, but the ballet suffered from its reputation as an aristocratic bauble. Alexandre Benois recalls that in his childhood, "ballet was considered unworthy of the attention of serious people," and that "one of the chief reproaches made against the Tsar's Government was that it patronised and encouraged the ballet" (1941, 47–48).

Pushkin immortalized the dancer Istomina and Didelot's ballets in *Eugene Onegin* (I.18–21) in the 1830s, but by mid-century – already the period of high realism in Russian literature – the ballet's failure, or inability, to address the contemporary socio-political situation in Russia had come to the attention of Russia's intellectuals. In 1863, Saltykov-Shchedrin wrote:

> I love ballet for its constancy. New governments rise up; new people appear on the scene; new facts arise; whole ways of life change; science and art follow these occurrences anxiously, adding to or sometimes changing their very compositions – only the ballet knows and hears nothing. . . . Ballet is fundamentally conservative, conservative to the point of self-oblivion.
>
> (1935, 7: 132–133)

Three years later the poet Nikolai Nekrasov published "Ballet," a verse indictment of the Russian ballet and its public, in the February 1866 issue of *Sovremennik* [*The Contemporary*], Russia's leading literary journal.

The task of responding to either realism, nationalism, or the social questions troubling Russia in the nineteenth century presented the imperial ballet with a number of obstacles. Saltykov-Shchedrin censured the ballet the same year that a group of nationalist painters known as the Wanderers seceded from the Academy of Arts and societies for the advancement of Russian music were already established in both capitals. But an art form with origins in Renaissance court spectacle could not easily exchange its aristocratic protagonists for peasant ones, as the revolutionary ballets of the early Soviet period have shown, and the inclusion of Russian national dances only exacerbated the situation (Krasovskaya 1963, 10). As late as 1902, Petersburg balletomanes reviled Aleksandr Gorsky's naturalistic production of *Don Quixote*, which abandoned the nineteenth century's traditional hierarchical notions of ballet costuming and staging.

Despite the fact that they represented more a symptom than a cause of the ballet's malaise, the Petersburg balletomanes, the favorite target of realist writers' attacks on the ballet, remained the most visible and powerful sector of the ballet's public. Benois, writing about ballet in Russia in the 1870s and 1880s, cites several reasons for the general anti-ballet and anti-balletomane sentiment among the "serious public" of his childhood:

> The *balletomanes* formed a special clan of their own and had the reputation of being hopelessly incorrigible cranks; they were looked upon as somewhat eccentric and slightly depraved. Besides, in this epoch there prevailed in Russian society ideas of an utilitarian and materialist kind, born of the social movement which marked the beginning of Alexander II's reign. These ideas found expression in the aphorism of the time: "Boots come before Pushkin." It was only natural that from such a puritanically materialist point of view, the ballet (which did not preach anything "useful," where nothing for the improvement of society was advocated, and people were only busy with such nonsense as dancing, and in very scanty costumes at that) was considered unworthy of the attention of serious people. . . .
>
> We must not forget that up to the assassination of Alexander II a majority of the intelligentzia and even members of the highest circles, though not really at one with the extremists or nihilists, were, nevertheless, in warm sympathy with liberal ideals, and therefore considered it their duty to take an attitude of opposition to the government wherever and whenever they could. I felt that ballet was appreciated in a lesser degree than opera or drama, and that grown-ups talked about it in the same vein as when they spoke of the circus or the operette.
>
> (1941, 47–48)

A more serious impediment to creating a Russian national ballet remained the problem of the ballet master. Since its inception in 1738, the imperial ballet school had produced scores of talented Russian dancers, but ballet masters continued to be hired from abroad, as were leading dancers, designers, conductors, and composers. The presence of foreigners on the production staff of the imperial theaters was felt most acutely when Baron Karl Karlovich Kister was appointed Director of Imperial Theaters in 1875. The balletomane and critic Konstantin Skalkovsky portrays Kister as a most unpopular figure in St Petersburg, a reputation his near-total neglect of Russian art had earned him. Skalkovsky's assessment of Kister is dismissive, yet representative of the vociferous press his appointment generated:

"He wasn't able to understand 'Russian' art, since in essence he was a foreigner" (1899, 12). Skalkovsky quotes A. S. Surovin regarding the general crisis in the theater repertory under Kister's management: "This German baron in Russian art played the role of a gardener in an *orangerie*, who, having no luck with flowers, planted cabbages and potatoes instead" (ibid., 9).

Ivan Vsevolozhsky

Baron Kister's replacement, Ivan Vsevolozhsky (1835–1909), had his own difficulties with Petersburg's balletomanes, but theater professionals admired his administrative policies, his knowledge of the theater, and his taste. Obituaries and appreciations of the director published after his death in 1909 cite the ascension of Alexander III to the throne and his appointment of Vsevolozhsky to the theater directorate as the beginning of the "new era" in Russian theater (Krivenko, Boretsskoi). Karl Valts, who served sixty-five years in the imperial theaters had only praise for him:

> I. A. Vsevolozhsky was perhaps the most helpful director of the theater in the whole time of my service. A cultured, enlightened person, who, in addition to a subtle understanding of art, also possessed a sharp critical mind that penetrated all the details of everyday life in the theater.
>
> (1928, 128)

Vsevolozhsky was made director of the imperial theaters in 1881, having spent the previous five years in the Russian consulate in Paris, where he presumably developed some of the qualities his successor, Vladimir Telyakovsky, ascribed to him:

> He was a real *barin* (gentleman), with the tastes of a European and the cunning of a diplomat. He was never sincere, however, and not distinguished by his temperament, and for that reason, though he basically loved the theater, he was not carried away by it. The main purpose to which he strove was to please the court – and not to be carried away by any extremes.
>
> (1965, 30–31)

Vsevolozhsky's "foreign tastes" provoked the ire of proponents of nationalistic Russian art and culture, but despite the controversy surrounding his appointment, Vsevolozhsky was an effective director. The reform movement he initiated shortly after his appointment continued for two decades (culminating in the disturbances in the theaters and theater institutes during the socio-political upheavals of 1905). Some of these reforms were aimed at modernizing the theaters and increasing their efficiency: warehouses were built and archives established. Other reforms responded to artistic problems as repertories came under the scrutiny of special committees. The most far-reaching of these reforms was the lifting of the state theaters' monopoly in 1882, a move that did much to revitalize the Russian stage in the next decades.

Private theaters and foreign artists in Russia

With the repeal of the prohibition against private theaters in Russia, the imperial theaters were suddenly – and for the first time in their long existence – forced to compete for audiences. The general increase in theatrical activity in the capitals benefited the imperial theaters in the long run, however. The presence of touring companies accelerated the reform of the state theater, and in many cases, talent discovered and nurtured in experimental theaters enterprises found its way to the imperial stages.[18]

Although ballet in Western Europe was in a serious state of decline by 1882,[19] the appearance of European dance companies in Russia influenced both the production of ballets and the dancing on the imperial stages, and began to attract a new public to the ballet. Petersburg audiences could now see whole troupes of visiting artists on the private stages (notably those in suburban amusement parks) opening in and around St Petersburg – a flood of foreign dancers compared to the trickle of ballerinas formerly invited to appear on the imperial stages. Petipa's incorporation of the Italians' brilliant point technique in his choreography (and subsequently, into the syllabus of the Russian *danse d'école*) was one of the first direct results of the repeal of the state theaters' monopoly.

French academic technique formed the basis of the Russian school of dancing from its inception in the 1730s. The vast majority of the ballet masters working in Russia had been schooled in that technique and passed their training on to their Russian pupils. The first significant departure from this pattern occurred in the 1860s, when Christian Johansson, a protégé of Bournonville, began teaching in the school and introduced Danish technique to the Russian syllabus. Although Bournonville (like Petipa) had studied with Auguste Vestris in Paris, the syllabus he developed in Copenhagen stressed fleet articulation of the feet, and greatly expanded and refined the male dancer's academic technique. The tours of Italian ballerinas in the

1880s and 1890s heralded the next appreciable foreign influences on the Russian school: advances in female point technique.[20]

The Italian school's bravura technique depended on strong feet to perform an array of virtuosa *pas* on point. Matilda Kshesinskaya, one of the first Russian ballerinas to master that technique (she studied with Enrico Cecchetti) and to take over the roles Petipa had choreographed for the Italian virtuosi, recalled (somewhat immodestly) the personal impact of Virginia Zucchi's appearances in Russia:

> I was fourteen when the famous Virginia Zucchi arrived in St Petersburg. . . . From the day that Zucchi appeared on our stage I began to work with fire, energy and application: my one dream was to emulate her. . . . The result was that when I left the School I had already a complete mastery of technique.
>
> (1961, 26–27)

Kshesinskaya's quick mastery of the new technique testifies both to the solid technical foundation the Russian school had given her and the speed with which the Italian technique was incorporated into the Russian ballet syllabus.

By the end of the nineteenth century, the Russian school of dancing represented an amalgamation of dance styles and techniques, combining the grace of the French school, the filigree of Danish footwork, and the technical brilliance of Italian dancing with the upper-body refinement of its own tradition. Epaulement, the placement of the upper torso in opposition to the legs and hips, represented the uniquely Russian contribution to what became a distinctly Russian style of dancing. This slight twisting of the upper body represents an important stylistic refinement, a finishing touch to otherwise "square" positions of the French school.

The ballet-féerie

While the Italian style of dancing was quickly adopted on Russia's imperial stages, the vehicles in which the Italians appeared were greeted with considerably less enthusiasm. The *ballet-féerie* was the dominant Western dance genre in the 1880s and the one that found its way to the private stages in Russia. Fairy tales typically provided the plots of these productions and lent the genre its name, but the common denominator of féeries remained their emphasis on visual spectacle. A popularized version of the grand ballet, the féerie exaggerated the worst features of Petipa's productions: visual effects completely overshadowed the choreography; the dancing emphasized flashy virtuoso numbers for the stars and precision routines for the corps de ballet. A compromise of opera house and music hall aesthetics, the féerie was the predecessor of the showgirl "revues" and "follies" of the turn of the century.

The most famous of these works was Luigi Manzotti's *Excelsior* (1881), a ballet which depicted the triumph of civilization over the spirit of darkness. The contest played out in such unlikely locales as Volta's laboratory on Lake Como, the Central Telegraph Office in Washington, DC, and the Brooklyn Viaduct in New York City. Against this backdrop of Industrial Age kitsch, ballabiles and pas de deux allegorically depict such elevated notions as civilization, invention, force, science, and agriculture.

Excelsior premièred in St Petersburg in 1887 on the stages of two amusement parks simultaneously. The outdoor theaters of the Arkadia and Livadia parks presented the majority of the féeries in Petersburg, including danced versions of *Around the World in Eighty Days*, *A Midsummer Night's Dream*, and the operetta *Voyage dans la Lune*, in which Virginia Zucchi made her Russian début. Benois' recollections of the dancing from that work give an idea of both the artistic and production values of these presentations:

> Zucchi was dancing accompanied by a small *corps de ballet* and a very indifferent partner; she represented some fantastic creature who could as well be imagined at the bottom of a moonlit sea as in the garden of the Hesperides. The ballet had nothing in common with the rest of the operette. It was just a choreographic number, devoid of subject or drama. . . . Towards the end of her dance she rose on her points and, taking tiny steps, began gliding backwards to the music of a very popular song, *Nur für Natur*.
>
> (1941, 76)

The féeries did not present a serious threat to the imperial ballet's hegemony, yet their influence was felt in both the choreography and production of ballets for the imperial stages in the 1880s and 1890s. Slonimsky's catalog identifies *The Magic Pills* (1886) as Petipa's first féerie, followed by *Sleeping Beauty* (1890), *The Nutcracker* (1895), and *Bluebeard* (1896) (1971, 383–386). Vazem cites an earlier work, *Bandits* (1875): "[The ballet] was doubtless suggested to Petipa by féeries" (1937, 162). Petipa was quick to utilize the new Italian technique in his later works as well. The great roles from the last period of Petipa's work in the Maryinsky (Aurora in *Sleeping Beauty*, Odette in *Swan Lake*, and *Raymonda*) were all choreographed for Italian ballerinas and designed to exploit their technical proficiency.

It would be a mistake to assume that Petipa's féeries were wholesale

19

appropriations of the genre, or that his choreography for the Italian virtuosi resembled the *pas* they danced in Manzotti's spectacles, however. Much of Petipa's genius as a choreographer rested in his ability to assimilate new techniques and genres in his works without compromising the identity of his choreography. Petipa adamantly defended "his" theater and its traditions in an 1896 interview on the subject of the Petersburg ballet:

> Ballet is a serious art form in which *plastique* and beauty must dominate, and not all sorts of jumps, senseless spinning and the raising of the legs above the head. That is not art, I repeat once more, but a clown act. The Italian school is ruining ballet. It corrupts the public, turning it away from serious ballet and accustoming it to féeries, which are being introduced on the ballet stage by men like Manzotti, for example, who has delivered a féerie – yes, not a ballet, but the féerie *Excelsior*. In Paris they've already stopped giving grand ballets and content themselves only with small ones. There the ballet is dying, absolutely dying. And there's no one to support it. . . . The Petersburg ballet is not dying and won't die as long as the influence of the Italian school isn't felt.
>
> (*Peterburgskaya gazeta*, 2 December 1896)

Petipa's remarks reveal his deep ambivalence to both the féerie and the Italian school – even as he continued to borrow from the genre for his own ballets and choreograph for féerie stars engaged by the imperial theaters.

The repeal of the ban on private theaters in Russia and the arrival of dance troupes from abroad served as a kind of checkup for the Russian ballet, exposing both the strengths and weaknesses of an organization that had functioned in relative isolation since its inception. Clearly, the ballet had fallen behind the increasingly rapid pace of Russian cultural life by the end of the century. Other problems, like the technical inferiority of Russia's ballerinas, came to the attention of the public only after the Italians' arrival.

Still, Petipa was correct in heralding the achievements of his company. The abridged ballets staged in Paris and the Italian féeries provided a fairly reliable measure of the ballet's decline in Western Europe at the time the production capabilities of the imperial ballet continued to expand. The production of *Sleeping Beauty* in 1890 provided a more accurate gauge of the imperial ballet's standing. The ballet put the company's resources to a test whose successful completion marked the beginning of a new creative phase in Russian ballet that continued well into the next century.

2

SLEEPING BEAUTY: BALLET-FÉERIE AS *GESAMTKUNSTWERK*

T HE 3 January 1890 première of *Sleeping Beauty* and the gala dress rehearsal which preceded it by one day could not have been more auspicious, falling as they did on the first days of the nineteenth century's final decade. The ballet about a princess who awakens to find herself transported to the next century bode well for those who sought parallels between life and art. That the princess' name was Aurora and the action of the ballet moved from an atmosphere of social upheaval (the wicked fairy Carabosse not only intrudes upon the ballet's court festivities, she brings them to an end) to a dazzling Versailles-like court could only drive these meanings deeper. Ironically, the Aurora that would play a decisive role in Russia's fate was a battleship, not a princess, and the new dawn she heralded bore considerably more resemblance to the epoch of Louis XVI than of Louis XIV.

If *Sleeping Beauty* failed as a socio-political allegory, its promise for the history of Russian ballet was more than fulfilled. The ballet bridges two distinct eras in the history of dance in Russia, at once summarizing the achievements of the past century in adapting and refining a foreign art form and simultaneously indicating a new direction for the future of Russian ballet. *Sleeping Beauty* links the period of Russian ballet's relative obscurity outside a small circle of Petersburg elites to a second period, when Russian ballet gained an international, popular audience.

The work was conceived and created by a distinguished triumvirate: Ivan Vsevolozhsky, Marius Petipa, and Pyotr Tchaikovsky. Vsevolozhsky, then the director of the imperial theaters, oversaw the production. His involvement with the imperial ballet (from 1881) inaugurated a new creative phase in Petipa's choreographic career. Although Petipa had staged some fifty ballets for the imperial theaters by 1890, *Sleeping Beauty* provided the ballet master with his first opportunity to choreograph to a score composed for him by a first-rate Russian symphonic composer.[1] *Sleeping Beauty* was the first of three Tchaikovsky ballets staged at the Maryinsky, but the only one to involve Petipa and Tchaikovsky (as well as Vsevolozhsky) in a truly collaborative process.[2]

The Perrault tale and the romantic ideal

On 13 May 1888 Vsevolozhsky wrote to Tchaikovsky with an idea for a ballet he hoped Tchaikovsky would compose for the Maryinsky:

> I thought I would write a libretto to Perrault's *La Belle au bois dormant*. I want to do the mise en scène in Louis XIV style. Here one could bring musical fantasy into play and compose melodies in the spirit of Lully, Bach, Rameau, etc., etc. There absolutely must be a quadrille of all of Perrault's tales in the last act. It should have Puss in Boots, Tom Thumb, Cinderella, Bluebeard, and others.
>
> (Vsevolozhsky 1956, 169)

Vsevolozhsky had discussed the possibility of a new ballet for the state theaters with Tchaikovsky as early as 8 November 1886, when the composer met with Vsevolozhsky, Petipa, and Aleksandr Frolov, a ballet administrator (Tchaikovsky 1923, 110). They eventually decided on a ballet on the subject of Undine. Roland Wiley interprets Vsevolozhsky's 13 May 1888 letter as a tactful change of subject on the part of the director after a year and a half of procrastination on the part of the composer (1985, 103–104). Tchaikovsky's response to Vsevolozhsky's libretto is dated 22 August 1888:

> Je ne suis ici que pour quelques heures; mais j'ai eu le temps de parcourir le scénario et je tiens à vous dire tout de suite que j'en suis charmé, enchanté au-delà de toute description. Cela me convient parfaitement et je ne demande pas mieux que d'en faire la musique.
>
> (1974, 509)

The decision to base a ballet libretto on the Perrault tale, with music, choreography, and design in the style of the period of Louis XIV (and Perrault) would do nothing less than alter the course of Russian ballet. The usual "stylizations" of Russian nineteenth-century ballets bordered on exoticism, rather than authenticity. Locales such as India, Spain, and ancient Egypt offered visually arresting scenery, provocative costuming, and a measure of local color in the music and the choreography. But the music, design, and dance of France's grand siècle were familiar to Tchaikovsky, Vsevolozhsky, and Petipa in a way that the particulars of India and ancient Egyptian culture could not have been. The correspondents' enthusiasm for the period reveals both a knowledge and an admiration of French court culture that would yield a reasonably authentic homage to the court of Louis XIV. Vsevolozhsky imagined music in the style of Louis XIV's contemporaries, Lully, Bach, and Rameau, and dances in seventeenth- and eighteenth-century forms. To the extent that the collaborators' intentions were realized, *Sleeping Beauty* represents the first attempt to authentically stylize each component of an imperial ballet production.

Although his name appears nowhere on the *affiche* announcing the ballet's première – not even for the costumes he designed – there is general agreement that the libretto of *Sleeping Beauty* was written by Vsevolozhsky, as his 13 May 1888 letter to Tchaikovsky suggests: "I thought I would write a libretto to Perrault's *La Belle au bois dormant*." The idea to base a ballet on Perrault's fable was Vsevolozhsky's, and it was he who saw the project to fruition, making him the ballet's producer, as we understand the term today. Benois, in his reminiscences, describes the director's role:

> Chief credit for the triumph of resuscitated traditions belongs to Vsevolozhsky. Although the costumes invented by him could be criticised for their rather helpless amateurishness, he was the person responsible for *creating this masterpiece*, for he made the production of the ballet his own personal work. It was he who, by entering into all the details, became the link as well as the head of the whole production – a feature indispensable in the creation of a *Gesamtkunstwerk*. This resulted in a coherence and polish hitherto unseen.[3]

(1941, 131)

Vsevolozhsky was not the first ballet librettist to use Perrault's tale. Eugene Scribe had fashioned the libretto for Jean Aumer's 1828 Paris version of *La Belle au bois dormant*, which was restaged in London in 1833. Slonimsky maintains Vsevolozhsky was familiar with the "libretto, music, and iconography" of that ballet: "This is easy to ascertain in comparing the costume sketch of the evil fairy of the French ballet with the costume sketch of Vsevolozhsky's Carabosse" (1956, 173). Vera Krasovskaya lists other treatments of the Perrault tale on Western European ballet stages (1963, 292–294), but both Soviet historians agree that the ballet's libretto was derived primarily from the original Perrault tale.[4]

Vsevolozhsky's libretto represents an ingenious attempt to reconcile the structural demands of the Petipa grand ballet (as it had evolved from the tragic, two-act romantic ballet) to the essentially optimistic portion of Perrault's tale he chose to dramatize. The prolog and three acts of the ballet each center around a critical moment in the princess' life: christening, début, first love, marriage. This coming of age plot plays out against the background of the ballet's larger theme: the struggle between good and evil that the Lilac Fairy and Carabosse personify.

Like the tale, the ballet has six good fairies who bring gifts to the princess and one evil, uninvited fairy who curses her. In the tale, the youngest fairy (who grants the princess beauty) opposes the seventh, old and forgotten fairy and modifies the latter's curse. In the ballet, these become the Lilac Fairy and Carabosse. The titles of the variations for the remaining fairies combine their names and attributes: *Candide*; *Coulante, Fleur de farine*; *Miettes qui tombent*; *Canari qui chante*; *Violente*. The gifts they bring to the princess are never mentioned directly in the libretto, although the choreography of their individual variations, their names, and their musical accompaniment suggest that these fairies are also patterned loosely after Perrault's. The ballet's "Canary" fairy, for example, recalls Perrault's fifth fairy, who gives the gift of bird-like song. But her dance, which mimes its flute accompaniment, recalls the sixth, who gives the princess the ability to play musical instruments.

Vsevolozhsky abandons all but the high points of Perrault's *La Belle au bois dormant* after the ballet's prolog.[5] The events which follow – Aurora's prick with the needle, Désiré's vision of Aurora, the kiss, the wedding – fit the template of late nineteenth-century ballet structure as it developed from the romantic ballet: narrative sequence culminating in a mad scene, vision scene, resolution, divertissement. That formula was not unfamiliar to either the director or the choreographer, as Petipa had restaged an unprecedented number of the old romantic works in St Petersburg during Vsevolozhsky's tenure: *Giselle* in 1884, *Le Diable à quatre* in 1885, *Esmeralda* in 1886, and *La Sylphide* in 1892. In 1882 Petipa choreographed the dances for the St Petersburg staging of Meyerbeer's *Robert le Diable*, the opera that initiated the lyric theater's fascination with romanticism in Paris in 1831.

The structural similarities to these romantic works, especially *Giselle* and *La Sylphide*, become apparent in the first act of *Sleeping Beauty*.[6] Aurora makes her first appearance in the ballet in Act I when she arrives at her twentieth birthday party to find four suitors awaiting her. She dances with each of them in the Rose Adagio, but declines to choose a fiancé from among them. As in the prolog, a confrontation between the good and evil forces brings the first act to a close: Carabosse tricks the princess into dancing with the spindle that pricks her and begins the century-long sleep. Carabosse then disappears and the Lilac Fairy returns to watch over the kingdom.

The spindle prick and the princess' "death" are analogous to the scene of madness and death that typically ends the main narrative passage of a nineteenth-century grand ballet and occasions the vision scene that follows. But Petipa eschews the hysteria and disheveled appearance that characterize Giselle's mad scene. Aurora's "madness" is conveyed in purely classical terms. Listless, imprecise footwork precedes her collapse – a controlled undoing befitting a Princess Royal.

Prince Désiré is discovered hunting in the forest in the ballet's second act. Like Aurora, the prince must choose a mate, and the suite of dances that follows, for duchesses, marchionesses, countesses, and baronesses, serves the dual function of providing opportunities for the corps de ballet and demonstrating the depths of the prince's *ennui*.

The Lilac Fairy appears in a boat of mother-of-pearl after the hunting party departs and conjures a vision of Aurora and her friends. Based on the traditional *ballet blanc*, the scene shows choreographic similarities to ballet's most famous vision scene, the second act of *Giselle* (1841), which Petipa had staged in Petersburg in 1884, and revived in 1887. But the vision scene of *Sleeping Beauty* differs from Petipa's previous white scenes in its mood and narrative function. The *ballets blancs* of *Giselle* and *La Bayadère* mourn lost heroines; the vision scenes of ballets such as *Don Quixote*, or the "*jardin animé*" scene of *Le Corsaire*, are divertissements that do nothing to advance the narrative. In its combination of narrative function and choreographic form, *Sleeping Beauty*'s vision scene functions as a *ballet blanc* divertissement as well as a pas d'action. Like the vision scene of *Giselle*, it satisfies the need for a "pure-dance" episode that features the corps de ballet while it furthers the narrative, anticipating the ballet's dénouement.

Although the vision scene is set in a forest, like the corresponding scenes of *Giselle* and *La Sylphide*, the action take place in daylight. As her name implies, Aurora, unlike her romantic predecessors, is no spirit condemned to darkness. She represents the future, not the past, and potential rather than loss. Désiré has not come, like Albrecht, to atone for past philanderings, nor is his vision induced by opium as were Lord Wilson's (in *Daughter of the Pharaoh*) and Solor's (*La Bayadère*). The second act of *Sleeping Beauty* is ballet's first fully conscious vision scene.

The secondary characters are also positive projections of their romantic counterparts. The Lilac Fairy replaces Myrtha, the authoritarian presence in *Giselle*; the wilis, the bodily representation of her power, are replaced by Aurora's spectral friends. And where *Giselle*'s wilis pry their heroine from Albrecht and form impenetrable walls to contain him, the nymphs in *Sleeping Beauty* never admit their physicality. They too keep Désiré from his vision, but the barriers they form are abstracted barriers that suggest the difficulty – though never the impossibility – of reaching his ideal. Désiré passes through them as though treading water. When he finally reaches Aurora in the adagio of their pas de deux, her movement is a sinuous aria of escape.

The ballet concludes with a third-act wedding scene, Petipa's preferred justification for the final divertissement: wedding celebrations end *Don Quixote*, *Daughter of the Pharaoh*, *Camargo*, *Zoraiya*, *Bluebeard*, *Raymonda*, and bring about the tragic dénouement of *La Bayadère*. According to Vazem, "one of the favorite devices of the ballet master . . . was to stretch out the action to some kind of celebration, especially a wedding, in order to give full rein to the staging of various classical and character dances" (1937, 66). Foreign ambassadors dancing national and/or character dances typically populated these scenes. But *Sleeping Beauty*'s final act pays homage to Perrault and his epoch with its parade of Perrault characters and miniature choreographic accounts of several Perrault tales in the main divertissement.

Creating a golden age

The 1890s mark the beginning of a period of classical revival in Russian culture. Ballet, which survives only through the continual repetition of centuries-old precepts, was ideally equipped to recall its past even though the performing arts, unlike literature and the visual arts, lack concrete ancient antecedents. *Sleeping Beauty* introduced the foreign, "classical" origins of theatrical dancing to the Petersburg public in much the same way that many Russian artists would begin to revive classical themes in their work.[7] As a result, the ballet of the French court of the seventeenth and eighteenth centuries came to represent a golden age of ballet in late nineteenth-century Russia, and provided a source of imitation, inspiration and innovation for those associated with the imperial ballet and the Ballets Russes for nearly four decades.

Louis XIV style

Louis XIV danced the role of the Sun King in *Le Ballet de la nuit* in 1653. The king made his appearance in the fourth and final section of a ballet consisting of forty-three separate entrées representing the twelve hours of night. Louis cast himself as the rising sun in this work, appearing with Aurora and accompanied by allegorical representations of honor, grace, love, riches, victory, fame, and peace (Kirstein 1984, 74–75). In their famous collection of caricatures of members of the imperial ballet (c. 1902–1905), Sergei and Nikolai Legat depict Pavl Gerdt, the company's venerable *danseur noble*, as the Sun King. In a frowzy wig, with the sun emblazoned on his chest, the stooped Gerdt offers a gentle parody of the long tradition of "noble" male dancers.

In choosing Louis XIV style for *Sleeping Beauty*, Vsevolozhsky referred not only to the zenith of the court ballet tradition, but also to the ballet's traceable origins. For lack of a workable system of dance notation, the historical memory of dance traditionally extends no further than a dancer's earliest lessons and teachers. In Petipa, a student of Auguste Vestris, the outstanding dancer of the eighteenth century, the traditions of French dance of the pre-revolutionary period were very much alive. And while Petipa was the most authentic repository of French culture in the Petersburg ballet, he was not the only one.[8] Vsevolozhsky's francophilia was legendary; his knowledge of French art and culture matched his admiration for the period, and contributed in large part to the success of the ballet's stylization. Writing about *Sleeping Beauty* years later, Benois credited Vsevolozhsky with the creation of this "highest achievement of the Russian ballet." For Benois, a self-styled retrospectivist, much of this achievement lay in its successful recreation of past epochs:

It was Vsevolozhsky's idea to contrast two different epochs, divided by a hundred years. . . . This "bridge," joining two centuries, gives the ballet a special poetical charm. The idea was executed by Vsevolozhsky with remarkable tact in the style of the days of Perrault himself. The more distant epoch was presented in a somewhat fantastic transformation; the period contemporary to Perrault was realistically historical.

(1941, 131)

Evgeny Ponomarev, who designed costumes and accessories for many of Petipa's ballets, discussed Vsevolozhsky's affinity for the period in an article he wrote on the director's designs for the imperial theaters which appeared in the turn of the century edition of the *Ezhegodnik*:

The content of this ballet allowed for a diversity of costumes, from the sixteenth century to the time of Louis XIV, in other words, the space of one hundred years. Here a deep knowledge of old French costume manifested itself, which the author of the drawings nourished with his obvious sympathy as well as the striking diversity of costumes and types of fantastic ballet personages.

(1898–1900, 26)

Vsevolozhsky's were not the only allusions to the French tradition in *Sleeping Beauty*, but they proved most accessible to the majority of those who wrote about the ballet. More than half of D. D. Korovyakov's review of the ballet concerns visual, rather than choreographic or musical details of the production. The reviewer offers an apology at the end of this lengthy section: "As you can see, in speaking about the new ballet, one must speak first and foremost about its staging, which, in fact, occupies a predominant place."

Korovyakov refers to the court of Louis XIV repeatedly in his review: "The hunt of Désiré (Act II) takes us right to the golden age of Louis XIV, with its mincing marquises and crimped cavaliers." He conflates the ballet's King Florestan XIV with Louis XIV, and refers to the ballet character alternately as "The Sun King" and "King Louis." *Peterburgskaya gazeta* reported audience confusion: "Those leaving the theater ask each other: 'Why is the king called Florestan XIV on the program, and not XII or XIII? In Perrault's original he's just "the king" ' " (4 January 1890). But Korovyakov's summary of the final act suggests the potency of Vsevolozhsky's redaction of Versailles: "The last act takes place on an esplanade, the décor behind it recreates a completely accurate large Versailles palace, with terraces, a fountain, a carousel, grand pièces d'eau and other luxurious effects of King Louis."[9]

The ballet's designs did not fail to impress the critics, though not always favorably. Yet the designers' adherence to period style went almost unnoticed. *Peterburgskaya gazeta* called *Sleeping Beauty* a "museum of theater props, and nothing more" (16 January 1890, 3).[10]

Archaisms in the choreography

The allusions to the court of Louis XIV in the ballet's décor, music, and choreography amount to much more than decorative or stylistic references to Versailles or gratuitous visual splendor; they refer to the classical dance's roots. The "floor show" entertainments at fifteenth-century French and Italian banquets were the predecessors of the earliest ballets, such as Beaujoyeulx's *Balet comique de la Royne*, staged in Paris in 1581 for Catherine de Medici. As dance performances moved from Renaissance banquet halls to modern proscenium stages in the seventeenth century, the syllabus of the classical ballet developed to best display the dancing body on the stage. Dance treatises written from the sixteenth to nineteenth centuries – Thoinot Arbeau's *L'Orchésographie* (1589), Pierre Rameau's *Le Maître à danser* (1725), and Carlo Blasis' *Traité élémentaire, théoretique et pratique de l'art de la danse* (1820) – show the development of the art from a primarily social, participatory enter-tainment to a professional theatrical activity: where Arbeau describes deportment and courtly etiquette as well as the social dances of his time; Blasis codifies the canon of a *danse d'école* similar to the one employed in the training of classical dancers to this day. The seventeenth cen-tury represents both the apogee of the court ballet (with Louis XIV its most visible symbol) and the turning point at which dance is transformed into a professional activity: Louis (who danced publicly from 1651 to 1670) established the first dance academy in 1661, the predecessor of today's Académie Nationale de la Musique et de la Danse, better known as the Paris Opera.

Still, Petipa's choreographic allusions to the old French tradition received much less critical attention than the ballet's design or even its music. Korovyakov noted them, although his accounts of the ballet's design and staging are much more detailed.

> The most interesting numbers, bearing the stamp of the epoch and the knowledge and taste of M. Petipa, are the farandole and the variations of the court ladies at Prince Désiré's hunt and the divertissement of the fairy-tale

characters in the final act. . . . The final coda and the sarabande seem very strange with the mazurka, whose place in Versailles is questionable. Skalkovsky also mentions "old French dances" and the concluding farandole.

(1890, 2)[11]

The national and social dances typically included in the final divertissement of a nineteenth-century ballet are found in Acts I and II of *Sleeping Beauty*. The dances in the second-act hunt scene refer to ballet's prehistory: they recall the ballet's origins in courtly dancing and deportment lessons. The farandole, the traditional Provençal dance included in the second act, was meant to erase the modern genre distinctions between social and stage, peasant and aristocratic dancing. According to Petipa's plan for the ballet, "a marquise proposes to dance a farandole like the local villagers" (1987, 280).

The court dances and the farandole of the second act furnish a clear choreographic contrast to the vision scene that follows: the setting of the ballet does not change, but the arrival of Aurora and the corps de ballet – and the strictly classical dances they perform – provide an element of otherworldliness. Their point shoes and dancing costumes by themselves illustrate the transformation of the art form over the previous century. The choreography of the vision scene, with its ethereal, romantic-ballet ballerina, completes the history lesson.

The ballet's most obvious tributes to French court culture are the processionals mentioned in Korovyakov's review. Two of these begin the prolog and final act, effectively framing the action of the ballet. The third concludes the ballet's final act. These processionals, or *entrées*, allude to the tradition of the *ballets à entrées*, which dates to the early part of the seventeenth century, at about the same time ballets began to be given for paying audiences in public theaters. Perceived as a corruption of earlier court ballet forms, the new genre was the forerunner of the *féerie*, anticipating its predominant visual effects and elaborate staging. The *ballet à entrées* consisted primarily of entrances and tableaux, whose variety furnished the work's chief interest. *Les Quatre Monarchies chrétiennes* (1635) featured twenty *entrées*, "depicting the various peoples of the world, each with their appropriate music and costumes" (Reyna 1965, 51). The *entrée* form was durable if not sophisticated, and provided the structures of later works such as Rameau's *Les Indes galantes* (1735), an opera-ballet with *entrées* for Turks, Incas, and American "savages."

In *Sleeping Beauty*, the *entrées* determine the structure of the prologue and third act and serve as the focal points of Acts I and II, where they introduce the main characters. Tchaikovsky's score indicates four separate *entrées* in the prolog: *Entrée des dames et des seigneurs, du Roi et de la Reine, des Fées, de la Fée des Lilas*. In the first act, the king and queen appear on the terrace, as do Aurora's suitors; the only *entrée* in this act is for the princess. The second act is structured similarly: the main *entrée* is for Désiré, who enters immediately after his hunting party.

Entrées comprise the entire third act of *Sleeping Beauty*. The opening processional, echoing the ballet's first in the prologue, is the "triumphal entry" of the king: *Entrée et Cortège du Roi et des Fiancés, salués par les courtisans*. The polonaise which follows is marked "*Cortège des Contes des Fées*." Contemporary productions of *Sleeping Beauty* typically parade the fairy-tale characters who dance the following numbers in this *entrée*, but the ballet's original libretto lists eighteen entrances. These include the first-act suitors, five of the seven fairies from the prologue, the fairy-tale characters who dance in the pas de caractères, pas berrichon, and pas de quatre, and Perrault characters who appear nowhere else in the ballet: Bluebeard and his wife, the Marquis de Carabas, Goldilocks and Prince Avenant, Donkey Skin (*Peau d'âne*) and another Prince Charmant, Beauty and the Beast, Cinderella and a second Prince Fortuné, Ricky of the Tuft and Princess Aimée, the Maneater and his wife (*Ezhegodnik* 1890–1891, 146–147). In the act's main divertissement, some of the participants in the polonaise reappear in character dances. The *entrée* preceding Aurora and Désiré's pas de deux – the main *entrée* of the ballet – is the only one in the score designated by its own number (28a). The final *entrée* of the ballet is a sarabande for Turks, Americans, Romans, Persians, and Indians, recalling Rameau's *Les Indes galantes*.[12]

The ballet concludes with another archaizing feature, an apotheosis staged as a *Gloire des Fées*: "Apollo in the costume of Louis XIV, lit by the sun and surrounded by fairies" (Petipa 1987, 284). This scene is not described in any version of the libretto, although Pleshcheev recounts the expected *tableau vivant*: "Another apotheosis was given in conclusion – a tableau vivant, depicting Apollo" (1896, 306). Petipa's preliminary sketches for the ballet include a longer description of the scene: "Apollo, as the Sun King Louis XIV. Fairies with long trains, as drawn on the ceilings of Versailles. . . . When [Apollo] personifies the sun, he has a cock on his shoulder and is crowned with rays of sunlight. Four white horses draw his chariot on which the signs of the zodiac are represented" (Wiley 1985, 156). Although Vsevolozhsky's designs for the ballet include the golden Louis XIV costume in which the Sun King was to appear, a photograph of the ballet's apotheosis scene shows Louis/Apollo and his entourage painted onto the backdrop, with the ballet's on-stage personnel posed around these pictorial representations (see Konstantinova 1990, opposite 64, 119). The ballet's final nod to Apollo is the first of a series of Russian ballet references to the Sun God and leader of the muses, an idea which received its definitive treatment decades later in George Balanchine's 1928 ballet *Apollon Musagète* (now titled *Apollo*).

The ballet's genre

Ballet-féerie *on the imperial stage*

As the title of this chapter suggests, *Sleeping Beauty* represented an uncomfortable fusion of nineteenth-century theatrical genres. Though Benois later described the ballet as a true *Gesamtkunstwerk* – a work that successfully fused its component parts into a coherent whole – the affiche for the ballet's première announced a ballet-féerie: an imported popular Western dance genre, typically relegated to the stages of St Petersburg's amusement parks. It was not the first *ballet-féerie* produced on the Maryinsky stage, but *Sleeping Beauty* – based on a well-known fairy tale and produced at enormous expense – galvanized critical opinion concerning the new genre in a way earlier *féeries* had not. The critic writing for *Peterburgskaya gazeta* [*Petersburg Gazette*] responded specifically to the work's genre designation: "*Ballet-féerie!* . . . A new word, used for the first time on *affiches*. But this word '*féerie*,' as a foreign word, fully suits the new ballet, the subject of which is taken from the *foreign* tales of Perrault" (quoted in Wiley 1985, 189).[13] The critic for *Peterburgsky listok* [*Petersburg Leaflet*] objected to the relationship of the ballet's choreography to its narrative:

> In order to produce a ballet that is a *ballet*, and not a *féerie* with dances, it is essential that: a) that the dances correspond to at least the elementary demands of the choreography, and b) that these dances are a direct consequence of the libretto of the work presented.
>
> [In *Sleeping Beauty*] the dances don't *illustrate* the action at all. The dances are stuck in for no reason, and in most cases come as a surprise, like a hair that has fallen into the soup. So the audience member who hasn't read the libretto beforehand or hasn't acquainted himself with the plot won't understand a thing.
>
> (5 January 1890)

This was not the first time a nineteenth-century lyric theater work was judged incomprehensible, nor would it be the last. (Lev Tolstoy's attack on nineteenth-century opera in *What is Art?* (1898) is quite similar.) In fact, the libretto of *Sleeping Beauty* ranks among the more lucid of nineteenth-century ballet narratives, with the story line concentrated in the early acts and its last scene devoted to the extended divertissement. But the critic's objections center around precisely that delineation of narrative and "abstract" dance.[14]

Aleksandr Pleshcheev raises similar objections, emphasizing the subjugation of dance to the *féerie*'s visual splendor:

> Balletomanes, and the lovers of choreographic art generally, were not happy to see the fusion of ballet with even such an elegant *féerie*, in which dance is only a supplement to the effects of the production, which play the leading role. Fortunately, our talented artist M. I. Petipa applied his full effort and created such a mass of choreographic masterpieces that the *féerie*, despite its unprecedented splendor, did not succeed in devouring the ballet. It would have been unthinkable to demand that the new fruit of M. Petipa's fantasy would be composed of something pithy and complete since the scenarios of all *féeries* are designed primarily around external effects and give almost nothing to mimed dramatic scenes, or generally speaking, to a performance in which mind and spirit could be invested.
>
> We saw a beautiful divertissement that had no less success than the remarkable décor and the magical metamorphoses. It would be wrong not to thank the directorate when it displays generosity for the production of a new meaningful ballet, but it is strange to make the choreography dependent on magnificence and transformations. Some take exception to this, they feel the ballet isn't lost, but going its own way, and that one form of art cannot undermine another. But the *féerie* cannot acknowledge even its related art form. What is more, it is taking over the repertory, squeezing out the ballet, which, in any case is left with only one day in the week. Looking at ballet as an art form – and the directorate does just that, since they even have a special school for the preparation of dancers – it is unfair to place it on the same level as the *féerie*. This reminds me somewhat of the invasion of the repertory of the Aleksandrinsky Theater by operetta, which was wisely forced out, despite its incredible success.

> (1896, 304–305)

Pleshcheev's remarks merit the lengthy quotation because they effectively summarize the debate concerning the *féerie*: the new genre subordinated choreography to visual effects and undermined the ballet's dramatic/expressive potential.[15] The *Peterburgskaya gazeta* writer peppered his review with similar reproaches: "No plot or dances!" "Don't even look for meaning!" (4 January 1890).

And most critics did not. Rather, the assemblage of costumes, properties, and scenery diverted attention from the true import of the ballet's brilliant staging:

> A great deal of taste and artistic talent was wasted on the production of the new ballet, to say nothing of the splendor of the costumes, which was taken to extremes. . . . Silk, velvet, plush, gold and silver thread, marvelous brocade materials, fur, feather and flowers, knightly armor and metallic decorations – it was lavish, price was not considered, even the costumes of the least important characters were lavish.
>
> (Korovyakov 1890, 3)

V. P. Pogozhev, director of Petersburg's imperial theaters, maintained that the wardrobe, machinery, and properties for *Sleeping Beauty* cost the imperial theaters 42,000 rubles "that is, more than one fourth of the entire yearly budget of the mechanical (that is, the production) section of the Petersburg theaters" (n. d., 51).[16]

Sleeping Beauty made use of a number of typical *féerie* stage effects: the transformation scenes, in which a forest "grows" to cover the castle and subsequently disappears; the moving panorama of the second act, which makes the Lilac Fairy's boat appear to sail. Korovyakov objected not only to their inclusion, but also their execution:

> We must admit that from the point of view of the scenic effects and the wonders of the mechanical section of our ballet stage neither the panorama nor the transformations pleased us. The movement of the cut panel between the public and the stationary boat, in full view of the stationary front plane of the décor gives a very weak illusion.
>
> (ibid.)

He concludes his review with an indictment of the ballet that echoes Pleshcheev's:

> If the ballet is going to be *only a spectacle*, a gay kaleidoscope of costumes and decorations, then no production will redeem it from vacuousness, emptiness, and that tedium that inevitably takes hold of all "adults," not to mention the aesthetically developed spectator.
>
> (ibid.)

The correspondent of *Syn otechestva* [*Son of the Fatherland*] was among the few who praised the ballet's combination of dance, music, and visual art, calling the ballet "a victory of art, combining in itself music, dance, and painting." The collaborative aspect of a production conceived and executed in the manner of Wagnerian opera was largely ignored by critics quick to identify the work's "low" genre origins. The Wagnerian aspects of the production would go unrecognized until the next generation of ballet collaborators would proclaim *Sleeping Beauty* a true ballet *Gesamtkunstwerk*.

Ballet as court spectacle

The *ballet-féerie* provided an obvious model for *Sleeping Beauty*'s elaborate staging, though there are a number of plausible motivations for the ballet's production. The ballet amounted to yet another of Vsevolozhsky's theater reforms, an attempt to raise the visual standard of the ballet to the new heights attained by work's choreographer and composer. And while it is true that *Sleeping Beauty* was based on a fairy tale and extravagantly produced, the goals of the production were antithetical to those of the typical *ballet-féerie*. *Sleeping Beauty* mined a rich lode of dance history and lore, recalling and creating, rather than destroying ballet tradition as its harshest critics maintained. Vera Krasovskaya sees the ballet as an attempt to revive French court theater:

> To Vsevolozhsky, such a ballet seemed quite different from a Western European dance revue, where a contemporary thematic predominated. He dreamed of something else – to revive the magnificent court spectacle of old France.
>
> (1963, 292)

Krasovskaya's suggestion is particularly interesting when read with Léon Bakst's recollections of the general rehearsal of *Sleeping Beauty*:

> An unforgettable matinée! I lived in a magic dream for three hours, intoxicated by fairies and princesses, by splendid palaces dripping in gold, by the enchantment of the fairy tale. . . .
>
> But what a return home! What a cruel end to the enchantment! Outside, deep gloom once more after those dazzling sights. A horrible driving snow, a glacial wind from the Neva, vain attempts to find a cab (too expensive near the theater), and finally, home: an oil lamp, sad and bourgeois, hung too high. . . .
>
> Oh! What a contrast to the Maryinsky, swathed in beautiful blue velvets and filled with dazzling officers of the guard and women in low-cut dresses, decked out, radiant. A perfumed, diverse throng in which the red uniforms and the white stocking of the court valets – so elegant, glittering with imperial eagles – introduced a solemn note.
>
> (1921, 1)

In describing the three worlds he inhabited in that afternoon, Bakst conflates the world of the performers and spectators in the Maryinsky. And the parallels suggest another possible motivation for the production of *Sleeping Beauty*: reminiscences of Vsevolozhsky suggest that the ballet might have been planned as a homage to the Russian court.[17] The two outstanding qualities that color contemporaries' accounts of Ivan Vsevolozhsky are his love for France – especially French culture of the time of Louis XIV – and his desire to please the court:

> I. A. Vsevolozhsky was a kind of courtier. He considered himself a marquise of the era of Louis XIV. . . . In Petersburg he recognized the ballet more than anything else because the tsar's family went there most often.
>
> (Gnedich 1929, 141–142)

> This was a real *barin* (lord) with the tastes of a European and the cunning of a diplomat. . . . His main goal was to please the court and not to go in for any extremes.[18]
>
> (Telyakovsky 1965, 30–31)

Vazem also portrays Petipa as an ambitious courtier:

> He tried by all possible means to make a career and to that end, to please the broad mass of the public, the theatrical directory, and most importantly – the imperial court. . . .
>
> Petipa always glanced over his shoulder at the imperial residence, vigilantly tracking the impression his ballets made on the imperial personages and the court dignitaries, whose opinions were the echo of their judgments, and hanging on their lips, tried one way or another to oblige their tastes.
>
> (1937, 62, 190)

These accounts suggest that the parallels Bakst noted in his memoirs were not entirely coincidental, that Vsevolozhsky (with Petipa) might consciously have planned the ballet as an elaborate tribute to the tsar and his entourage. Although such an interpretation is defensible, the ballet's libretto suggests otherwise. *Sleeping Beauty* clearly celebrates court life, but the court in question is hardly a model for emulation. In the ballet's crucial moment, the royal entourage stands powerless as Aurora dances with the lethal spindle, then waits for the fairies to arrive to settle the matter. The chief master of ceremonies, the character who invokes the wrath of Carabosse, is the model of the bumbling court sycophant, an unlikely inclusion if Vsevolozhsky had planned the ballet as a tribute to enlightened despotism, or wished to impress high officials, as Vazem suggests.[19]

A different view of Vsevolozhsky emerges from the memoirs of his theater colleagues. They describe an apolitical courtier, concerned primarily with the aesthetics, not the politics, of absolutist France. Karl Valts, designer and machinist of Moscow's Bolshoi Theater, admired Vsevolozhsky's culture, enlightenment, and critical mind (1928, 128). Alexandre Benois was fascinated by the director's anachronisms:

> Vsevolozhsky was the last survivor of the age of Catherine, although the year of his birth corresponds to the reign of Nikolai I, and all of his youth took place in the days of Aleksandr II. There wasn't even a hint of the "Nikolaevshchina" that left deep traces on the entire way of life of our great society. He didn't even resemble his contemporaries. He was the only one of them that could have participated with dignity at the Hermitage dinners of the Northern Palladium, in interviews with the crowned philosopher in Sans Souci, or at the meetings of the Marquis du Chatelet. Vsevolozhsky was raised in the·traditions of the eighteenth century, in a way of life in which the dance played such an important role, and for him dance was not something frivolous or absurd. . . . Thanks to his familiarity with dance, Ivan Aleksandrovich's gestures and especially his bows, were marked by a special refinement, even complexity, differing sharply from all the simplified American customs of our day.
>
> (1909, 2–3)

Another writer concurs with Benois:

> The Old Hermitage transported the old barin-Maecenas to the era of Catherine the Great, amidst the brilliant cavaliers and court ladies of yore. There in that circle even he – with his refined manners and his magnificent French pronunciation, with his surprisingly sharp witty words – would have been himself.
>
> (Krivenko 1909, 3)

Krivenko's allusions to Catherine II's Russia are particularly appropriate. In establishing the imperial theater system in 1756, Catherine played a role analogous to that of Louis XIV: Catherine's theater bureaucracy incorporated Petersburg's fledgling ballet school. The suggestion of Catherine II's world and the frequent allusions to eighteenth-century court culture in the descriptions of Vsevolozhsky provide a clearer picture of the world *Sleeping Beauty* conjured for its audiences. And although Benois discusses *Sleeping Beauty* as a work made possible by the socio-political situation in Russia at the turn of the century, his reminiscences suggest the importance of the history and traditions of the Russian ballet as well:

> *La Belle au Bois Dormant* is a typical production of Russian or rather St Petersburg culture. Nowhere else in the world could this fairy-tale have been

produced on the stage as it was in those days in the Maryinsky Theatre. To make this achievement possible, the coincidence of various factors in the mode of life of the country was essential: the aristocratic spirit, untouched by any democratic deviations, which reigned in Russia under the sceptre of Alexander III; the unique atmosphere of the St Petersburg Theatre School and the traditions that had been formed in consequence; and finally a rejuvenation of these traditions so that, on this occasion, shaking off the dust of routine, they should appear in all the freshness of something newly-born.

(1941, 130–131)

Benois is careful to identify the ballet with St Petersburg and the traditions of St Petersburg's ballet academy, and he credits the country's autocratic, aristocratic spirit for the work's success. St Petersburg – the birthplace of Russian secular culture, the nexus of historical tradition and political power – would become a central symbol in Russia's burgeoning modernist movement, and the ballet that trafficked so fully in those ideas would in turn play an important role in the revival and re-appraisal of the Russian capital in the next phases of Russian modernism.

In her book *Sleeping Beauty*, Marina Konstantinova explores the ballet's connections to St Petersburg, using the imperial city and its royal palaces as central metaphors for the ballet:

Before us a cosmos of palaces and parks, rivers and seas, of slow ceremonial processions and splendid masked balls is gradually revealed . . . but all this refers not only to Petersburg as a place, but as a spiritual focus of Russian history from the time of Peter I, so that a reference to that history often expresses itself precisely in this relationship to St Petersburg.

(1990, 62)

For Konstantinova, the Lilac Fairy and Carabosse are none other than the forces of civilization and nature, waging their pitched battle over the fate of the historical city. The courtiers in the ballet find themselves caught in the midst of this struggle, in the same way that Pushkin's civil servant in "The Bronze Horseman" must weather the flood that threatens to overwhelm the Russian capital. In retelling this most basic Petersburg myth – nature's immanent threat to the "unnatural" city – the ballet's creators celebrate the city and the forces that combined to create and sustain it. "In the Petipa/Tchaikovsky ballet, as in the structure of the city of St Petersburg, the harmonious architectural cosmos vanquishes the chaos of the destructive, raging elements" (ibid.).

Konstantinova's "ballet as palace" metaphor serves as a multivalent symbol of the work's implications for the history of Russian ballet and culture. The work pays homage to the art form's origins in the royal courts, to the imperial patronage that supported it, and to the ballet's vaunted position in French and Russian court life. *Sleeping Beauty* celebrates the aesthetics of daily life – not the politics – of the grand siècle in its recreation of the period's décor, dance, music, and courtly manners. But there is no evidence to suggest that the ballet was consciously staged by Vsevolozhsky to gain court favor.

The ballet's revival of Louis XIV style initiated new interest in Russia's own grand siècle, prompting a renaissance of historical St Petersburg in Russian arts and letters. The Tchaikovsky–Vsevolozhsky production that followed *Sleeping Beauty*, the opera *Queen of Spades* (1890), paid homage to Catherine II's Russia with much music adapted from the period (including a *gloire* to Catherine), a pastoral interlude, and an aged countess who recalls her youth in ancien régime France. These works sparked a fascination with the historical imperial city – the cradle of Russia's secular arts – though the implications of *Sleeping Beauty*'s tribute went largely unrecognized at the ballet's première. Konstantinova called Petersburg "a blind beauty . . . not recognizing itself in its own brilliant portrayal. There was an unfortunate justice in this, for it was difficult to make out the entire magical perspective of the ballet/palace while standing so close to it" (ibid., 121).

The legacy of *Sleeping Beauty*

Sleeping Beauty was a box-office success despite decidedly mixed reviews,[20] so popular that Tchaikovsky's brother Modest had trouble obtaining a seat one month after the première:

> Yesterday I tried to get a ticket from scalpers, but even there everything is sold out. Counting the last (eighth) performance, the total profit at the box office was thirty thousand rubles. . . . I asked Vsevolozhsky yesterday to provide a box for me for at least one performance, and imagine, I was refused. All the boxes and stalls are already taken . . . your ballet has become a kind of obsession. Guriev told me today that people have ceased saying to each other "How are you?" Instead, they ask, "Have you seen *The Sleeping Beauty?*"
>
> (Smakov 1989, 22)

The following season, *Sleeping Beauty* accounted for 21 of the 45 ballet performances given in the Maryinsky. During the 1891–92 season, the ballet was performed 12 times; in 1892–93 it had 15 performances.

The popularity of the ballet and the unusual number of performances it was given help to account for the rather high incidence of those subsequently involved in the history of Russian ballet who claim to have seen it. Many of them recall the production as the one that most influenced their ballet careers. For Alexandre Benois, the critic André Levinson, Anna Pavlova, and Igor Stravinsky, who saw the ballet not long after its première, the ballet was a *coup de foudre* (see Benois 1941, 123–132; Summer 1982, ix; Money 1982, 3; Goldner 1973, 284). Like many other Ballets Russes dancers who appeared in the ballet as children, George Balanchine cited the ballet as a turning point in his career: "Thanks to *Sleeping Beauty* I fell in love with ballet" (1985, 31).

The revival of classical aesthetics in Russian modernism is *Sleeping Beauty*'s legacy. That legacy can be traced through four decades of Russian ballet, from the retrospectivism of *Sleeping Beauty* to the "neoclassical" aesthetic of George Balanchine. The next stage in this development can be seen in the ballets Petipa and Vsevolozhsky produced for the Hermitage Theater at the turn of the century and the early work of the Mir iskusstva group.

The "1900" ballets

Vsevolozhsky, the person most responsible for *Sleeping Beauty*, was made director of Russia's court theater, the Theater of the Imperial Hermitage in 1899.[21] (It would be difficult to imagine a post more in keeping with Vsevolozhsky's background, affinities, and character.) His removal from the Directorate of the Imperial Theaters marked the effective end of Petipa's work in the Maryinsky as well.[22] In the decade following *Sleeping Beauty*, Petipa oversaw the Maryinsky productions of Tchaikovsky's *Swan Lake* (1895) and *Nutcracker* (1892), choreographed several new ballets (including *Raymonda* (1898)), and restaged a number of older works. But the court theater became the chief venue for Petipa's choreography after Vsevolozhsky's transfer to the Hermitage.

In 1900, Petipa choreographed four short works that premièred in the Hermitage Theater in January and February and entered the Maryinsky repertory days later: *Ruses d'amour* (given in the Maryinsky as *The Trials of Damis, or Mistress into Maid*), *Les Saisons*, *Les Millions d'arlequins*, and *Les Elèves du Dupré*. Aleksandr Glazunov, who composed *Raymonda*, wrote the music for the first two ballets. *Les Millions d'arlequins* was composed by the imperial theaters' ballet conductor Riccardo Drigo. The last ballet was a reworking of *The Cavalry Halt*, an 1886 full-length ballet composed by Albert Vizentini.

These ballets continued the line of ballet anachronism begun with *Sleeping Beauty*. The *Ezhegodnik imperatorskikh teatrov* (The Yearbook of the Imperial Theaters), published by the directorate of the imperial theaters, documents the reliance on historical models in these productions. A Nicolas Lancret reproduction appears near the beginning of the summary of the 1899–1900 St Petersburg ballet season with the caption "Nira (A picture that served as a model for the décor of the ballet *The Trials of Damis*)." A reproduction of Pyotr Lambin's décor for the ballet's first act follows, verifying the ballet's adherence to its eighteenth-century example.[23] The music for the ballet boasts a similar pedigree: Glazunov's score begins with a dance adapted from Arbeau's *Orchésographie* (1598). Old French dances follow: "Le Passepied," "La Courante," "La Musette," "La Sarabande," "La Farandole," "La Gavotte pressée," "Variations du temps de la Comargo" (*sic*), "La Fricassée." Glazunov's use of archaic musical forms is discussed in the same edition of the *Ezhegodnik*. The composers cited in the author's discussion of Glazunov's archaisms (Bach, Lully, Rameau) are the same as those Vsevolozhsky recommended to Tchaikovsky in his 13 May 1888 letter regarding the composition of *Sleeping Beauty*.

> The gavotte, the sarabande, the farandole reveal the author's worship at ancient altars. "I mostly consider myself a classicist" he often says. It is no wonder that the composer has prepared himself for the musical incarnation of the style of Watteau as for a sacred rite, having thoroughly studied Bach, Rameau, Lully. The future will tell if he is called to revive the *Ballet de la Reine*.
>
> (Koptyaev 1900, 58)

Les Saisons, the second Glazunov ballet of the 1900 Hermitage series, is described as an "allegorical" ballet, representing the four seasons choreographically in the manner of a *ballet à entrée*. Drigo's *Les Millions d'arlequins* was a harlequinade, another standard eighteenth-century genre, which featured a cast of *commedia dell'arte* characters (Cassander, Columbina, Harlequin, Pierretta, Pierrot, Leander). Orest Allegri's second-act backdrop (reproduced in the *Ezhegodnik*) resembles an early Renaissance stage with perspective vistas. The costumes were humorous adaptations of seventeenth-century dress, with ruffled collars, buckled shoes, and large hats.

Still, the most overt of these homages to French court dancing was certainly *Les Elèves de Dupré*, whose eponymous ballet master was Louis Dupré, the eighteenth-century French dancer and teacher of Vestris and Noverre. The last two were included in the cast, as were the dancer Camargo, Louis XV, and Madame de Pompadour (danced, appropriately, by Petipa's daughter Maria). Like *Ruses d'amour*, the ballet featured a number of old French dances: gavotte, chaconne, gaillarde, allemande, passe-pied, passacaille.

The correspondent for *Novoe vremya* [*New Times*], reviewing *Ruses d'amour*, discussed the work's grand siècle allusions (its archaic dances, its plot drawn from Lamartine) and described the work as a painting by Watteau (25 January 1900, 14 April 1900). When *Ruses d'amour* (along with *Les Saisons*) was revived in 1909, Svetlov pronounced the Camargo costume "authentic" (1909, 29). But reviews of the Maryinsky performances of the 1900 ballets were generally cool; most critics dismissed the ballets as pleasant trifles.

Lev Ivanov revived Petipa's 1872 ballet *Camargo* for the Maryinsky Theater the following year (1901). The cast of characters, which included Camargo and Vestris, was already familiar. The 1900–1901 *Ezhegodnik* survey of the ballet season for that year includes (in addition to the usual photographs of costumes and drawings of the sets of the season's new ballets) a costume design for *Camargo* identified as "from a watercolor of Boquet" and the eighteenth-century engraving on which the ballet's set design was based, again corroborating the production's authenticity to period style.[24]

These 1900 ballets revived major eighteenth-century ballet genres (the anacreontic comedic plot of *Ruses d'amour*, the harlequinade, the allegorical ballet) that had been largely subsumed by the grand ballet form. Harlequins, allegorical set pieces, and mythological characters were still featured in the divertissements of Petipa's "grand" ballets, but in the 1900 ballets, these genres were presented as such, not as diversions from the plots of evening-long narrative works. As they explored the origins of theatrical dancing, these ballets probed the ballet's non-narrative possibilities. *Les Saisons*, in particular, affirmed the expressive value of the dance itself, without reference to anything but the most basic "argument." In this respect, the ballets anticipate two main features of ballet production in the twentieth century: the tendency toward shorter works and the development of abstraction in dance.[25]

These ballets were not the first self-consciously retrospectivist ballets choreographed by Petipa. A similar series of ballets had been choreographed for the Peterhof court theater's summer "parade spectacles": *Les Offrandes à l'amour, ou Le Bonheur est d'aimer* (1886) was the first of these, followed by *The Awakening of Flora* (1894), an "anacreontic" ballet, *The Pearl* (1896 and 1898), and *Thetis and Peleus* (1897), a "mythological" ballet. It is no coincidence that these ballets were produced during Vsevolozhsky's tenure as Director of the Imperial Theaters, or that they followed Petipa's Petersburg revivals of several historically significant ballets: *Giselle* (premièred in Paris in 1841, revived in St Petersburg in 1884), *Le Diable à quatre* (premièred in Paris in 1845, revived in St Petersburg in 1885), *La Fille mal gardée* (premièred in Bordeaux in 1789, revived in St Petersburg in 1885). There is little precedent for this type of historical revival in Petipa's work prior to Vsevolozhsky's tenure, nor did deliberately anachronistic works comprise a significant portion of the pre-Vsevolozhsky–Petipa œuvre. *Camargo* and *The Adventures of Peleus* are the notable exceptions to a long line of original Petipa ballets produced for the Petersburg Bolshoi and Maryinsky theaters which traffic in Spanish, Oriental, or generically exotic themes.

But in the hands of Petipa and Vsevolozhsky, the legacy of *Sleeping Beauty* became a series of increasingly hermetic variations on the theme. The recreation of the court spectacle, which *Sleeping Beauty* had so gloriously brought to life, became an end in itself. The ballets produced for the court theater were performed in a setting as anachronistic as the eighteenth-century stylizations themselves. Benois dismissed *Ruses d'amour* as "just a *bagatelle* suitable for a Court Gala in the Hermitage Theatre . . . the eighteenth century subject is graceful, but too light to be moving" (1941, 140). Where *Sleeping Beauty* presented the court of the grand siècle in all its splendor for the Petersburg public; the later ballets were choreographic miniatures, anacreontic trifles designed as aristocratic diversions.

Sleeping Beauty *and Mir iskusstva*

If *Sleeping Beauty* marked the beginning of the creative end for Petipa and Vsevolozhsky, it demonstrated the ballet's potential as an art form to the generation of Russian aesthetes grouped loosely around the journal *Mir iskusstva* [*The World of Art*]. Though a latecomer, Sergei Diaghilev became the unofficial leader of the *miriskussniki*, a circle that had formed already in a Petersburg gymnasium.[26]

Benois leaves a detailed account of his circle's association with ballet, beginning with his own infatuation with *Sleeping Beauty*. Although initially seduced by the ballet's retrospectivism, a Mir iskusstva hallmark, Benois and his circle recognized the ballet's innovations and capitalized on them in their brief association with the imperial theaters and later with the Ballets Russes. Benois identifies *Sleeping Beauty* as the important turning point that altered his career and the course of Russian ballet:

> Interest in the ballet, which had been somehow declining, was suddenly regenerated with fresh vigour and has never lessened since. It can be said with confidence that, had this production not proved to be such an outstanding success, the whole history of the ballet in general – not only that of the Russian ballet – would have been totally different. The *Ballets Russes* themselves would never have seen the light of day had not the *Belle au Bois Dormant* awakened in a group of Russian youths a fiery enthusiasm that developed into a kind of frenzy.
>
> (1941, 127)

Benois' love for the ballet developed slowly, over several viewings, fueled primarily by his admiration for the score:

> One of the great attractions of *La Belle au Bois Dormant* was the historical reminiscences that it evoked. No music had ever so successfully resuscitated the distant past as was done in the hunting scene and in the last divertissement of *La Belle au Bois Dormant*.
>
> (ibid., 124)

Nor was his appreciation for the ballet limited to its revivalism. In another account of his *Sleeping Beauty* experience, Benois hails the ballet as a total art work: "This was a time that I actually had the happiness to see a genuine Gesamtkunstwerk" (1980 I, 606). Benois repeatedly attributes the success of *Sleeping Beauty* to Vsevolozhsky: "It was [Vsevolozhsky] who, by entering into all the details, became the link as well as the head of the whole production – a feature indispensable in the creation of a *Gesamtkunstwerk*" (1941, 131).

Benois' preoccupation with *Sleeping Beauty* eventually led to the Mir iskusstva group's forays into ballet production. After a successful début as editor of the 1900 edition of the *Ezhegodnik*, Diaghilev was anxious to become involved in the planning of new works. In 1901, the new director of the state theaters, Sergei Volkonsky, reluctantly agreed to Mir iskusstva participation in a new production of the Delibes ballet *Sylvia*, a pet project of Benois, who dreamed of a "perfect" staging of the work.

The involvement of "outsiders" in imperial theater productions –

especially to the extent envisioned by Mir iskusstva – was quite unprecedented. Their essentially modern approach to ballet production – a Wagnerian attempt to synthesize the choicest ingredients – differed markedly from imperial theater practice, and shows the influence of Vsevolozhsky. Although outside composers for new ballets were more the rule than the exception by 1900, most other aspects of ballet production – especially concerning repertory and casting – were handled within the theater bureaucracy. And although *Sylvia* was never realized, the attempt foreshadowed Mir iskusstva involvement in the group's most famous enterprise: the Ballets Russes.

Petipa and Vsevolozhsky had been content to follow *Sleeping Beauty* with more eighteenth-century stylizations, but the Mir iskusstva group adopted the production methods and standards Vsevolozhsky pioneered and applied them to different periods and locales. Their ballets continued to privilege visual design over music and choreography – as had *Sleeping Beauty* – but the productions were planned with the lessons of that ballet and the idea of the *Gesamtkunstwerk* clearly in mind.

3

BALLET RUSE:
THE
DYING SWAN

M IKHAIL FOKINE'S 1907[1] ballet *The Swan* (better known as *The Dying Swan*) remains one of ballet's more persistent icons. The choreography consists solely of an endless stream of tiny steps on point and the delicate arm/wing flailings of a water bird in the throes of death. The imagery is hardly original — the full-length Petipa–Ivanov *Swan Lake* (1895) should have exhausted the woman-as-bird movement vocabulary. But Fokine's ballet focuses on the swan's death, a moment his predecessors had chosen to leave unchoreographed.

In truth, *The Dying Swan* is not a ballet, but an encore, a twentieth-century "new" ballet response to the conventions of the Petipa ballet (now deemed "old"). The old ballet's martyred heroines were real girls with mothers, suitors, friends, and rivals. Even *Swan Lake*'s eponymous heroines are women under a spell, and the ballet's narrative focuses on their human concerns. Fokine's swan has no story. The choreographer adapts the full-length ballet's stylization, while omitting its narrative pretext. The pathos of Fokine's choreography lies in this muteness; death is presented as such, without motivation or consequence.

That blend of beauty and pathos helped make the brief *pièce d'occasion* the most enduring and frequently performed of Fokine's works. Maya Plisetskaya, the great Bolshoi Theater ballerina of the 1950s and 1960s, continues to perform *The Dying Swan*, heedless of the ballet's ironic potential.[2] Susan Jaffe, a dancer with the American Ballet Theater, rendered the work for a nationally televised variety show celebrating George Bush's presidential inauguration (1989), restoring in one stroke the aura of high-art kitsch that must have attended Pavlova's own performances of *The Swan* in provincial vaudeville theaters and second-floor opera houses.

Fokine's *Swan* – brevity notwithstanding – is a study in excess, a calculated tear-jerker whose self-parody lurks below the surface of each performance. Yet the work furnishes an apt metaphor for the new ballet's deleterious effect on the nineteenth-century ballet academy. In staging the demise of the nineteenth-century ballet's most potent symbol, Fokine distilled the artistic decadence that characterized the twentieth-century's new ballet into the several minutes Saint-Saëns' "Swan" requires.

The Swan amounted to a manifesto of the new ballet: no longer would the titillations of the old ballet (the mad scene, the sexually suggestive pas de deux) cloak themselves in the larger framework of lofty goals and elevated sentiments. The new ballet focused on the old ballet's emotional peaks, liberating them from the constraints of nineteenth-century ballet form. The ballet "*bien fait*," only recently evolved, was effectively truncated in favor of a more organic assemblage of expressive parts.

The devolution of the academy

This chapter discusses the so-called "new" ballet (a term used to distinguish the choreography of Fokine, Gorsky, and Nijinsky from that of the school of Petipa) as a decadent phase in the history of Russian ballet. This period of decline, which began with Petipa's late ballets (*c.* 1900) and continued into the 1920s, is typically celebrated as the acme of the Russian ballet's achievement. In her book *Era of the Russian Ballet*, Natalia Roslavleva, like most writers on this period, regards the first decades of the twentieth century as the Russian ballet's "heyday" (1966, 167). Lynn Garafola claims that "in the history of twentieth-century ballet, no company has had so profound and far-reaching an influence as the Ballets Russes," the Russian ballet's standard-bearer in this period (1989, vii). But the legacy of this supposedly vital period is remarkably small. Of Fokine's eighty-odd works, less than ten have come down to us. Only one of Nijinsky's ballets has been preserved in an unbroken tradition, and Gorsky is represented in the modern repertory chiefly by his restagings of Petipa's ballets.[3]

What is more, the creative phase of this period of Russian ballet history was remarkably brief. By 1913, the year that Nijinsky's *Le Sacre du printemps* leveled the most serious attack on the academy, the creative burst of the early years of the Ballets Russes had run its course. With the loss of many of the Ballets Russes' original collaborators during and after the First World War, neither the quality nor the originality of the first seasons could be maintained.[4]

While writers on this period typically characterize it as the one in which the ballet emerges in the artistic vanguard, at last joining forces with her sister art forms, it is important to remember that the new ballet was merely the latest manifestation of a constantly evolving tradition. The chapter examines the developments of the new ballet in light of that tradition, evaluating these supposed advances in that context.

There is inherent irony in labeling the dance of the early Russian modernist period "decadent." The word, invoked so often against Russian modernists of all stripes at the turn of the century, had become something of a cipher by the time Soviet critics adopted it to disparage unofficial art. The common denominator of those twentieth-century applications concerns a turn from the various academic and high-art traditions of the previous century.[5] Here, the term will be used to describe a turn from the ballet academy, from the ballet's basis in the *danse d'école*, and an increasing reliance on the other elements that comprise the ballet spectacle: music, décor, drama, props.

The period of decline was too brief to have a decisive effect on the Russian *danse d'école* – the imperial ballet school continued to produce capable technicians.[6] But ballet lives only in performance. And as the ballets produced in those years demanded increasingly less of their interpreters and audiences, the Russian ballet's brush with outright popularity nearly resulted in the loss of its soul. At least in performance, the ballet's nineteenth-century academic tradition was very nearly cast aside.

Not long after the academic style reached its peak with the production of *Sleeping Beauty* in 1890, Petipa began repeating that ballet's formula – with mixed results. His 1900 ballets, *Ruses d'amour*, *Les Saisons*, *Les Millions d'arlequins*, and *Les Elèves du Dupré*, were stylized homages to the golden age of court ballet. Created for the court theater, these ballet miniatures presented their audiences with privileged looks at authentically stylized, archaic dance genres. But these were purely retrospectivist works, museum pieces that broke no new artistic ground.

Their premières in the Hermitage court theater (rather than in the Maryinsky Theater, Petersburg's primary dance venue) were the first of several omens signaling the end of the Petipa era in the history of Russian ballet. Petipa was 81 by the time those works were presented; his assistant, Lev Ivanov (who choreographed *Nutcracker* and the second act of *Swan Lake*), died the following year, leaving the ballet master without a seasoned protégé to continue to choreograph in his own style. In 1902, Aleksandr Gorsky's Moscow version of *Don Quixote* replaced Petipa's in the Maryinsky repertory and Nikolai Legat, a promising, though inexperienced young choreographer, was made Petipa's assistant. In 1903, after the successful première of the Legat ballet *Die Puppenfee*, Petipa was retired, leaving the St Petersburg ballet essentially without a head.

Petipa's departure dealt a serious blow to the Russian ballet academy. To most minds, Petipa *was* the academy, the embodiment of the Russian *danse d'école*, as Valerian Svetlov (1911, 3) suggested: "The Petipa ballet was academic and the sum of his work has given us a true academy of ballet." In truth, the Petipa academy represented the only viable national dance academy in the early years of this century, a fact confirmed by the Imperial Theater Directorate's unsuccessful attempts to replace Petipa with another European ballet master in 1902.[7]

Although the imperial ballet never recovered fully from its losses in the first years of the century, the success of the Diaghilev ballet seasons offset the disorder and stagnation in the state theaters. By the time the deaths of Vsevolozhsky and Petipa (in 1909 and 1910, respectively) marked the definitive end of the imperial ballet's period of greatness, Russian ballet had attained instant celebrity in Europe under Diaghilev's aegis. And even though Petipa and Vsevolozhsky had anticipated some of the theatrical innovations of the next decade and century (retrospectivism, a Wagnerian emphasis on the unity of the production), the imperial theaters would have a difficult time meeting the rapid pace of innovation in the Russian arts in the 1900s, much less take the lead, as the Diaghilev ballet would do in those years.

The ballets of this period, generally regarded as the artistic zenith in the history of Russian ballet, would seem to have little in common with Petipa's retrospectivist ballets (even though the four 1900 ballets set the tone for the revivalism that would characterize Russian ballet in the coming decades). Nor did the company that presented them much resemble the main venues of Russian dance a mere ten years later. To speak of Russian ballet in 1900 was to speak of the imperial St Petersburg ballet, with its attached school, ballet master, scenic artists, and composer/conductor. By the time of the revolution, that tradition had fragmented, with leading exponents of Russian ballet performing primarily in Europe, in a company whose production wing included both Russian and European artists and composers. In less than two decades, Russian ballet evolved from a local, imperially sponsored company and school to one which incorporated a variety of separate styles, techniques, and performance traditions.

Retrospectivism in Russia's fin de siècle

For all the stylistic disparity of the ballets produced in the first decades of the twentieth century – both in Russia and by Russian companies abroad – retrospectivism remained their common denominator. Their revivalism took two primary forms. Levinson describes the first of these as a kind of "contemporary hellenism," an infatuation with the art of ancient Greece. The second celebrated neoclassicism: usually French but increasingly Russian as well.

Russia's "new" ballet trafficked in both types. Fokine's "antique" style, characterized by such ballets as *Acis and Galatea*, *Eunice*, *Narcisse*, and *Daphnis and Chloë*, found its primary inspiration in Isadora Duncan's pseudo-Greek stylizations. Fokine's cohorts, Aleksandr Gorsky and Vatslav Nijinsky, also choreographed ballets on Greek themes (Gorsky's *Salammbô* and *Eunice and Petronius*, Nijinsky's *Faune*). French neoclassical homages played an important role in Petipa's last creative period (notably in *Sleeping Beauty* and ballets produced for the court), yet none matched the quantity or quality of Petipa's 1900 series of eighteenth-century stylizations, the stylistic antecedents of several of Fokine's own retrospectivist works: *Le Pavillon d'Armide*, *Le Carnaval*, and *Chopiniana* (given in the West as *Les Sylphides*).

The new ballet's stylizations rapidly achieved the status of gimmicks rather than innovations, however. Elizabeth Suritz writes: "The ballet developed so swiftly in those years, seizing and incorporating any discoveries, so that in the case of *Narcisse,* [Fokine, 1911] the critics already wrote about the 'usual repertoire of antique movements'" (1977, 347). By 1900, the correspondent for *Novoe vremya* described *Ruses d'amour* as representative of a genre "that has come into fashion here even in the provinces" (14 April).

Contemporary hellenism

The imperial ballet's homages to eighteenth-century French ballet (*Sleeping Beauty*, *Ruses d'amour*, etc.) established early precedents for Russia's fin de siècle retrospectivism, but the hellenism of Russia's decadent/symbolist writers proved the more important influence in the development of Russia's "new" theater (and subsequently, its "new" ballet) in the 1900s. In "The Old and New Ballet," published in the 1913 *Ezhegodnik*, the critic André Levinson wrote:

> The providential or perhaps, fatal trait of our contemporary culture is that in our hope of either the renewal of form or of content, we turn our gaze to Ancient Greece. The words "that's how it was with the Greeks" possess an incomparable fascination and conclusiveness for us.
>
> (1913a, 3)

Friedrich Nietzsche's popularity in fin de siècle Russia accounts for much of this fascination with Greek antiquity. *The Birth of Tragedy* began to be read in Russia by about 1890 (Rosenthal 1986, 10), the year of *Sleeping Beauty*'s première. Although Nietzsche's influence may be seen in virtually all areas of Russian turn-of-the-century art and culture, literary artists document the philosopher's impact most clearly. George Kalbouss discusses the influence of Nietzsche's *Birth of Tragedy* on Russian symbolist drama:

> In *The Birth of Tragedy*, Nietzsche's identification of Apollonian and Dionysian trends in Greek drama provided a framework that the symbolists could adapt to advocate a revival of theater in Russia. Virtually all of them were interested in re-infusing drama with a religious spirit as found in the Dionysian and medieval mystery plays.[8]
>
> (1986, 183)

The paradox of the symbolists' hellenism lies in their advocacy of classical themes while eschewing classical values. Symbolist discussions of classical art all but disregard the apollonian principle. Evelyn Bristol observes that "Ivanov's preoccupation with Nietzsche focused immediately on the Dionysian cult" (1986, 150).

The symbolist drama and theater that emerged at the turn of the century provided an antidote to the perceived excesses of Stanislavsky's naturalistic Moscow Art Theater,[9] which had barely established its company style when the symbolists began to attack its productions. The landmark production of Chekhov's *The Sea Gull* [*Chaika*] was staged in 1898, and by 1902 Valery Bryusov had fired the first round in the battle for the "ideal theater" of the future. Bryusov closed his essay, "Unnecessary Truth" (published in *Mir iskusstva*) with a call to arms: "I summon you from the unnecessary truth of the contemporary stage to the deliberate conventionality of the ancient theater" (1902, 74). Nikolai Vashkevich's "The Contemporary Dionysian Theater: A Sketch on the Synthesis of Art" (1905) echoed Bryusov's call. Vashkevich, a former Art Theater actor, stressed the religious aspect of the ideal theater of the future: "The theater should return to its primitive roots in festival and worship" (ibid., 14–15). Bryusov advanced his theory of "the conditional theater" in "Realism and Convention on the Stage" in the collection *Theater: A Book about the New Theater* (1908), which included articles by Meyerhold, Sologub, Chulkov, and Bely and amounted to the collected manifestos of the new movement. At nearly the same time, Vyacheslav Ivanov published essays advocating Nietzsche's "Dionysian" theater in the journal *Vesy* [Libra]: "Wagner and the Dionysian Drama" (1905), "Nietzsche and Dionysus" (1908).

The anti-naturalistic theater advocated by Bryusov, Ivanov, Meyerhold, and others found its choreographic analog in the dances of Isadora Duncan, who gave her first performances in St Petersburg late in 1904. Isadora's dances appealed to the advocates of the new theater for a number of reasons. First, her movement idiom was largely self-taught and free-form, a perfect dionysian antithesis to the rigors of the nineteenth-century ballet's apollonian *danse d'école*. Second, the public received her dances as antique artifacts, despite their obvious unauthenticity and the fact that Isadora preferred to discuss them as dances of the future, not the past (Levinson 1911a, 42–43).

Levinson discussed Isadora's dance, the hellenism of 1900s Russia, and the art of the English Pre-Raphaelites as clichéd, popularized forms of classicism, designed to appeal to the public, but stopping short of a break with conventional art:

> If in her art there is no genuine continuity with the poorly-understood essence of the ancient theater, then its content, or even its moral basis coincides in part with the rather simplified and vulgarized hellenism of our day, whose banner is bodily freedom, the cult of plastic, tangible beauty – a cult nourished on beautiful museum recollections.
>
> (ibid., 43)

Based on static pictorial or sculptural images of ancient Greek friezes, vase paintings, and sculpture, Isadora's dances were necessarily unauthentic. The Swiss movement theorist Emile Jaques-Dalcroze pointed out their shortcomings: "It is . . . not enough for the modern dancer to reproduce certain decorative classical attitudes – which, in the Greek orchesis, would merely indicate pauses – in order to resuscitate and rhythmicise the life that animated classical dancing" (1921, 171). Levinson voiced similar objections to the use of static images as a basis for movement: "They are capable of fixing only a moment of the movement, chiefly its beginning or end" (1911a, 43).[10]

The plethora of "Greek" ballets in the repertories of the Petersburg and Moscow imperial ballets and in the Diaghilev ballet represented Isadora's most obvious Russian legacy. In the imperial theaters, where semi-nudity and free-form movement were not permitted, Fokine and Gorsky had to content themselves with approximations of Isadora's style and technique. But Isadora showed the way to other, more important innovations in Russian ballet. She demonstrated the possibility of producing and performing dances outside the academy, without the attendant companies, schools, or theater bureaucracies. More importantly, her dances struck at the heart of the art form: movement to music. Her use of "concert" music and unorthodox movement vocabulary challenged Russian dance artists to rethink the most basic definitions of their art.

Valerian Svetlov (1909, 39) judged Isadora's conception of the dance's unity her most important contribution to the art form: "[in their] inseparability from the music, meaning, and the costume of the artistic moment, the dances are not a mechanical recreation of conventional technical methods, but a rhythmic and inspired emotional experience of what is being portrayed." Isadora's passionate works revealed some of the expressive shortcomings of Russian ballet in the early 1900s, and the most acclaimed ballets of the early Diaghilev seasons – *Schéhérazade*, *Polovtsian Dances*, *Spectre de la rose* – were indebted to the degree of emotional depth with which Isadora infused her performances.

Bals poudrés

The hellenism championed by symbolist dramatists and Duncan had a powerful, if relatively brief, impact on Russian theater and dance. Its influence would gradually be subsumed by the classical revival that members of the Mir iskusstva group continued to promulgate. From 1898 until 1904 the journal *Mir iskusstva* functioned as the primary venue for the various retrospectivisms its contributors championed: mainly French and Russian neoclassicism, but also the art of Ancient Greece and early *Rus'*. In the years that followed, dance and the visual arts – the fields most closely linked to Mir iskusstva – produced the bulk of Russian art's eighteenth-century tributes. And following the precedent set by the 1890 production of *Sleeping Beauty*, the ballet remained the most important retrospectivist venue.

But interest in past epochs extended far beyond the realm of Russia's artists and historians. The abundance of Petersburg charity balls on classical and neoclassical themes in the ten years leading up to the 1917 revolution suggests a broader, public interest in the cultures of past epochs (and an unlikely response to the Russian symbolists' calls for a "new" theater that would break down barriers between performer and audience).

Imperial theater artists frequently performed at these theme parties despite a prohibition against public performances outside the state theaters. Maria Petipa, outfitted as Diana, sold champagne at an "Artists Ball" in 1900. The ball had a Greek theme and costumes one newspaper termed "decadent" (*Novoe vremya*, 14 February, 3).[11] In March 1908, Fokine and Benois produced a short harlequinade, *The Swindled Guest*, for a "*Bal poudré*" in Louis XV style. Krasovskaya sees the seeds of the ballet *Carnaval* (1910) in that work (1971, 224, 229). The Fokine–Benois collaboration that eventually entered the repertory of the Diaghilev ballet was first shown at a 1910 ball given by the journal *Satirikon*.

Fokine fashioned more French dances for a "Bal chez Louis XIV" in 1911, though the most far-reaching of these divertissements was clearly "The Evening of Terpsichore," staged by Fokine in the Maryinsky Theater in January 1908. *Peterburgskaya gazeta* printed an interview with Fokine to publicize the event: "dances of the past, present, and future will be represented in the form of a review." Fokine described a lengthy program, to feature dances from ancient Egypt, Rome, Greece, and ancient *Rus'*, grand siècle France, and national dances from Italy and Hungary. Anna Pavlova was to impersonate Marie Taglioni in an authentic costume ("in appropriate makeup and a long skirt"). Contemporary ballet would also be represented, "by ultra-modern dances with pirouettes, etc. . . . finally it will be time for a 'matchish'[12] and dances in the style of Duncan. . . . For the first I think I'll invite a Negro . . . Mme Kyaksht will interpret the Duncan genre." When questioned about the lack of dances from the Middle Ages, Fokine responded that many of these dances "have no documentation. . . . Others simply aren't interesting to watch" (1971, 223). The lack of documentation for the greater share of Fokine's program would indicate that the latter consideration far outweighed the former.

A similar blurring of entertainment and history occurred in the dramatic theaters in the 1900s and 1910s, the most overtly pedagogical event being Nikolai Evreinov's "Ancient Theater," an enterprise that produced two seasons of historical plays, giving French medieval plays in the 1907–1908 season and Spanish Renaissance dramas in 1911–1912. The imperial theater production of Molière's *Don Juan* (1910) culminated a series of eighteenth-century stylizations directed by Vsevolod Meyerhold. Znosko-Borovsky described the production: "The idea was to convey the atmosphere of the triumphal performances at Versailles, and many details of the productions of that time were maintained to give a sense of court life under Louis XIV." (1925, 305–306). Benois' review of the play carried the title "A Ballet at the Aleksandrinsky" (*Rech'*, 19 November 1910, 3).[13]

Of course, Diaghilev's Ballets Russes produced several series of retrospectivist ballets throughout its twenty-year history, from the Fokine–Benois *Armide* in the first Paris season to Balanchine's *Apollo*, to which the term "retrospectivism" hardly applies. In dance, as well as in literature and the visual arts in Russia, retrospectivism in its many twentieth-century guises would show the way to the future through the past.

The new ballet

Theater: The Book of the New Theater, a collection of essays published in 1908, gave a name to Russia's new, non-naturalistic, "conditional" theater. Dance writers were quick to adopt the terminology to distinguish the works of ballet innovators such as Gorsky and Fokine from those of their predecessors, even though in dance, as in the theater, the designation began to be used as the strength of the new movement had already begun to ebb.[14] The titles of works published from 1909 to 1911 indicate an increasing awareness of a new ballet style. Valerian Svetlov published his article "Thoughts on the Contemporary Ballet" in the 1909 *Ezhegodnik*. His book *The Contemporary Ballet* was published in Petersburg in 1911 and in French translation the following year. E. A. Stark contributed "The Ballet Renaissance" to the 1911 *Ezhegodnik* and Levinson repeatedly referred to the "new" ballet in the titles of his essays "On the New Ballet" (1911a), "On the Old and New Ballet" (1913a), and the book *The Old and New Ballet* (1918, trans. Summer 1982). The Paris correspondent for the journal *Apollon* cited historical precedents for the new ballet's revolt and sees in it a fundamentally new definition of the art form:

If Noverre rose up against the classical ballet of the seventeenth century, then Russian ballet represents a reaction against today's classical ballet with its stereotypical gauze skirts. Beginning with Duncan, going back to Wagner and blossoming from the primary trefoil of music, dance, and mime, Russian choreography affirms the new type of theatrical spectacle: a dual dance drama, epic and lyric.

(Turgendkhold 1910b, 12)

Gorsky's naturalism

Although Western audiences first became acquainted with Russia's new ballet through the works of Mikhail Fokine (known in the West as Michel Fokine), Aleksandr Gorsky paved the way for the greater share of Fokine's innovations. Originally a dancer in the Petersburg ballet, Gorsky (1871–1924) began staging Petipa works for the Moscow company in 1898 using a system of dance notation developed by and named after Vladimir Stepanov.[15] While in Moscow, Gorsky became acquainted with the developments on that city's dramatic stages at the turn of the century, notably those of Stanislavsky's Moscow Art Theater, and sought to apply them to ballet. He staged Petipa's *Sleeping Beauty* in Moscow in 1898 and *Raymonda* in 1900, but established his reputation as a ballet master with his own version of *Don Quixote* in 1900.

Gorsky's *Don Quixote*, renamed *Don Quixote of La Mancha*, testified to the influence of Moscow's theater reformers. Designed by the painters Konstantin Korovin and Aleksandr Golovin, both of whom had been involved in Savva Mamantov's private opera enterprise in the 1880s, the production aimed at a "naturalistic" staging of the nineteenth-century work. The backdrops portrayed somewhat realistic vistas of Seville, instead of the usual pastiche of perspective backdrops (forest, courtyard, palace interior) painted by imperial theater genre specialists. More importantly, the costumes were designed individually, in general color groups to harmonize with the colors of the set. Only the costumes for the female corps, whose dances were staged traditionally (in ensembles) were exempt. The emphasis on the individuals within the mass extended to the ballet's direction: Gorsky expected his dancers to analyze their characters' motivations for their actions on the stage. Stanislavsky's influence is clear, both in the cohesion of the production as a whole and the emphasis on its details.

The success of Gorsky's production in Moscow led to its transfer to the St Petersburg stage in 1902. That Gorsky's ballet was staged in Petersburg while Petipa (the work's original creator) remained the company's nominal first ballet master gives some indication of Petipa's standing in the imperial theaters in the years following Vsevolozhsky's departure. The production represented a challenge not only to the aging choreographer, but also to the Russian ballet academy he had fashioned in the fifty odd years of his tenure in Petersburg.

Even before the work was staged in St Petersburg, *Peterburgskaya gazeta*, the newspaper best representing local balletomane opinion, reported on the Moscow production:

> *Don Quixote* was staged in Moscow in the decadent manner. As an example, several dances were staged so that on one side of the stage they danced one way, and on the other side, to the same music, other dances were performed.
>
> (1 September 1901)

Gorsky responded to the charges in an interview in the same newspaper:

> Why decadence? . . . My production was distinct from traditional stagings in that there was continuous movement on my stage . . . I simply don't observe any kind of symmetry . . . the result is a varied spectacle, and the stage looks pictorial.

After the Petersburg première, *Peterburgskaya gazeta* published the artist N. Kranchenko's critique of the Korovin–Golovin designs: "It is impossible, not knowing perspective – neither spatial nor linear – to design for our best theater." The correspondent for *Novoe vremya* concurred: "In décor, and especially that of the artist Golovin, there is no perspective, no life, no clearly distinguishable colors; it seems that our decadents find that this is as it should be, that mood is necessary, but this mood is understandable only to a few" (22 January 1902). The reviewer, acknowledging Gorsky's pursuit of naturalistic "truth" in the production, did not find it. Rather, "the ugly spirit of decadence hung over the entire production."

Peterburgskaya gazeta's censure of the ballet responded primarily to the asymmetry of Gorsky's production – both visual and choreographic – rather than the actual dancing, as did the choreographer in his reply. The critics' charges and the choreographer's response illustrate the essential oppositions of the new ballet to the old. Symmetry and perspective remained fundamental principles upon which the art of ballet continued to be based. From the time of the Renaissance, the art had adapted to best exploit the possibilities of the lyric theater's perspective stages. And the compulsive symmetry of Petipa's compositions abetted the expansion of the romantic ballet's structure in the last half of the nineteenth century. In attempting to bring the ballet in line with the latest developments of Moscow's dramatic theaters, Gorsky and his designers abandoned this essential feature of the grand ballet. Petersburg's dance writers, staunch defenders of the academic tradition, were noticeably offended by the production's improprieties.

Gorsky's ballet, with its inchoate massed movement, represented a first step in the subversion of the classical dance academy. Although the *danse d'école* is generally regarded as a vocabulary of movement, these quotes demonstrate that in Russia at the turn of the century, the ballet's academy assumed a proscribed vocabulary of staging and presentation of movement as well. It follows, then, that Gorsky's attempt to undermine the traditional relationship between movement and space would become a familiar tactic of the new ballet (and a salient feature of Nijinsky's own assaults on the academy).

Gorsky followed *Don Quixote* with *The Daughter of Gudule* (1902), the ballet he considered his most successful (Krasovskaya 1971, 133). Like Jules Perrot's *La Esmeralda*, the ballet was based on Hugo's *Notre dame de Paris*.[16] In the best traditions of the Stanislavsky's Art Theater, Gorsky traveled to Paris to research the work. His libretto followed the novel as closely as possible, though Perrot had been content loosely to adapt the work's narrative highlights. The result was billed as a "mimo-drama," a drama in pantomime, rather than a ballet. Critical reaction to this innovation was predictably harsh: "The vain, naïve desire to *motivate* every dance movement gives evidence to the complete misunderstanding of the *extra-psychological* meaning of ballet" (Levinson 1911b, 160). Yuri Belyaev, writing for *Novoe vremya*, parodied Chekhov in protesting the Moscow ballet's "Stanislavization": "One wished to return home as quickly as possible. . . . To Petersburg! To Petersburg! To Petersburg!" (1971, 146).

Fokine's retrospective stylizations

Krasovskaya summarizes the goals of Gorsky's early stagings in her account of *The Daughter of Gudule*: "Gorsky was caught up in the noble goal of reforming the ballet spectacle according to the principles of realistic action, historical concreteness, and the avoidance of improbability and nonsense" (1971, 134). But Krasovskaya's characterization of Gorsky's early choreography could also be used to characterize the work of Michel Fokine (1880–1942), whose choreographic career began in St Petersburg in 1905. The early work of both choreographers represents a reaction to the academy's rigid notions of acceptability and convention. Both men attempted to do away with the conventions of the old ballet while buttressing the ballet's narrative possibilities. Both found solutions in the dramatic theaters.

The essential differences in their early choreography reflect the widely divergent theatrical trends in Moscow and St Petersburg in the first decade of this century. Gorsky's most important productions were staged in Moscow during the period of the Art Theater's first triumphs; Fokine's work in St Petersburg showed the influence of Isadora Duncan and vanguard theater director Vsevolod Meyerhold. Gorsky choreographed almost exclusively for the Moscow ballet, while Fokine attained early celebrity with the Diaghilev ballet in the West. The popular successes of the first seasons of the Ballets Russes belonged to Fokine: *Les Sylphides*, *Schéhérazade*, *Firebird*, *Le Spectre de la rose*, *Petrushka*.

Although Fokine's importance as a choreographer and innovator of the new ballet is well established, his role as a theorist of the movement remains controversial. Fokine suffered chronic anxiety of influence throughout his career, especially where Isadora Duncan was concerned. In *Michel Fokine and His Ballets* (1935), Cyril Beaumont's quasi-hagiographical account of Fokine's life and work (written with Fokine's cooperation and dedicated to him), Beaumont gives 1904 as the date of Fokine's first plan for ballet reform (ibid., 23). This manifesto took the form of explanatory notes attached to Fokine's scenario for the ballet *Daphnis and Chloë* (a ballet based on Longus and produced for the Diaghilev ballet in 1912). Beaumont then informs his readers that Duncan did not appear in St Petersburg until 1907.[17] In fact, Duncan performed in St Petersburg in 1904, at about the same time Fokine claims to have delivered his scenario and notes to Telyakovsky, then Director of Imperial Theaters.[18] Two extant copies of the scenario and notes were found by Yuri Slonimsky in preparation for his edition of Fokine's autobiography, *Against the Current* (1962/1981). The first of these was in the Fokine archive maintained in Russia by Fokine's brother-in-law, A. P. Krupitsky; the other was found in the archives of the ballet's composer, Andrei Kadlets (Roslavleva 1966, 174). While the scenario of *Daphnis and Chloë*, unrealized until the 1912 Ballets Russes production, has been generally accepted as a precursor to Fokine's 1905 ballet *Acis and Galatea* (ibid., 175), Vera Krasovskaya suggests a more plausible chain of events:

> Fokine backdated his scenario to 1904 in order to show his independence of Duncan. In addition, recalling his first ballet *Acis and Galatea*, given at the graduation performance on 20 April 1905, Fokine openly admitted: "Until then it hadn't occurred to me that I might have some ability in this area." The

entire account of *Acis and Galatea* corroborates Fokine's admitted lack of preparation for a ballet master's work and proves that the ideas expounded in the libretto of *Daphnis and Chloë* (1912) did not precede the production of *Acis and Galatea* (1905) but came later, not before 1907.

Then, in his memoirs, Fokine wished to shorten the time-span of his less successful endeavors. This is where the anachronisms unnoticed by Fokine occur, when the libretto of *Daphnis and Chloë* was attributed to 1904, and *The Dying Swan* was dated 1905 instead of 1907. All that was done earlier revealed in Fokine a gifted ballet master, but no special innovation.

(1971, 164)

Western writers on Fokine remain curiously silent on this issue.[19]

Fokine published two versions of his manifesto in 1916, after his break with Diaghilev. The first of these appeared in the Russian periodical *Argus*; the other in London's *Times*. The essence of the *Daphnis and Chloë* notes furnishes the core of these. The first discusses the "new" versus the "old" ballet; the second attempts to distinguish the Russian ballet (by which Fokine means the Diaghilev ballet then performing in London) from the "old" (nineteenth-century) ballet and from the work of Duncan. Both articles refine the principles of the new ballet Fokine claims to have set forth in 1904. Briefly stated, the dance should be interpretative and should express the epoch of the work in question; costumes should be appropriate to the theme and the music and movement harmonious; the ballet should represent a unity of music, painting, and dancing; applause should not interrupt the dance. Excepting the last, the principles Fokine proposed had already been put into practice in the works Gorsky and Duncan presented in St Petersburg in 1902 and 1904 respectively. Gorsky's *Don Quixote*, for example, represented an attempt to de-conventionalize ballet costuming and set design and blend the elements of the production into a more or less harmonious unity. Fokine's final principle, that applause should not interrupt the work, is a Wagnerian notion popularized in Russia by Stanislavsky's Moscow Art Theater.

Fokine choreographed his first ballet, *Acis and Galatea*, in 1905 for the imperial theater school. Over the next two years he authored several more works for students and a number of divertissements for charity performances both in and out of the imperial theaters. Fokine choreographed three ballets in 1907 that indicated the direction of his future choreography, and prefigured some of his most successful works for the Diaghilev ballet. *Eunice* and *Chopiniana* (later produced for the Ballets Russes as *Les Sylphides*) both premièred in the Maryinsky on 10 February 1907 at a benefit for the Gogol Society. *The Animated Gobelins,* choreographed for an imperial theater school performance, had its première in the Maryinsky on 15 April 1907. A longer version of the ballet was produced later that year for the imperial theaters as *Le Pavillon d'Armide*. Taken together, the three works attest to Fokine's early mastery of stylization. *Eunice*, a Greek ballet, showed the influence of Duncan and the Hellenism then in vogue in Russia. *Sylphides* and *Armide* are retrospectivist works, and belong in a line of ballets from *Sleeping Beauty* to Balanchine's *Apollo*, which have ballet classicism as their theme.

Fokine's contribution to the Russian repertory of grand siècle ballets was the brainchild of Alexandre Benois, who based *Armide*'s libretto on Théophile Gautier's "Omphale," a tale which fused E. T. A. Hoffman and rococo sensibilities. His libretto tells the story of a traveling viscount who takes refuge from a storm in the castle of an old marquis. The viscount rests in Armide's pavilion, an annex of the castle that houses a tapestry depicting her. While the hero sleeps, he dreams that the tapestry has come to life and he has become Armide's lover. When the viscount wakes, the marquis hands him the same scarf Armide had given him in the dream, now missing from the tapestry. He faints.

Benois and composer Nikolai Tcherepnin collaborated on *Armide* in 1900 and 1901. The imperial theaters accepted the work, but never produced it, owing to Benois' falling out with Telyakovsky, the new director. Tcherepnin had not completed the score, but the ballet's central scene had been orchestrated and performed in 1903. Fokine claims that he heard the work in concert and wished to use it (1981, 100); Benois maintains that Tcherepnin, then a conductor at the Maryinsky, recommended the work to the young choreographer (1941, 240–241). In any case, Fokine choreographed the extant scene for a 15 April 1907 school performance as *The Animated Gobelins*. The ballet's success led the theater directorate to produce the work for the imperial ballet. Benois wished to produce a full-length three-act ballet in the style of Petipa's grand ballets, juxtaposing pantomime and pure dance scenes according to nineteenth-century academic tradition. The theater directorate, no longer favorably disposed to evening-length works, insisted on a shorter version. Benois agreed reluctantly, and the ballet was produced in one act with three scenes.

The ballet's setting and décor link it stylistically to *Sleeping Beauty*, a work that served as a model for Benois and Fokine as *Armide* was being staged: "During my talks with Fokine I had insisted that he should always bear in mind first-class masterpieces like the scene in the forest and especially the last scene of *La Belle au Bois Dormant*, that contained the Versailles Sarabande and Prince Désiré's wonderful *variation*" (Benois 1941, 252). The ballet, like *Sleeping Beauty*, clearly celebrates the culture of seventeenth- and eighteenth-century France (the viscount's costume bears a strong resemblance to the Louis XIV costume Vsevolozhsky designed for *Sleeping Beauty*'s apotheosis). Benois' designs suggest his newfound admiration for Petersburg's own eighteenth-century court culture: Russian critics admired the ballet's revival of the "fairy-tale splendor of the Sun King's Versailles masquerades," but the French poet Jean-Louis Vaudoyer found the stylization closer to Peterhof than the Trianon (Krasovskaya 1971, 205). Diaghilev informed Benois of his intention to show the ballet in Paris after the 25 November 1907 première (1941, 266), and the ballet's blend of dance, drama, décor, and music served as a template for the ballets Diaghilev would later produce for his Ballets Russes.

Armide remained the curious blend of rococo and Romantic stylization that so appealed to Benois in his reading of Gautier. While Benois' décor and costumes were faithful to the age of the minuet, with panniers and jeweled turbans, the ballet's choreography and its score stopped short of authenticity, opting for stage-worthiness rather than naturalistic representation. Benois was enchanted with Tcherepnin's score ("It has been a long time since an 'orchestrated illustration' so appropriate to the action has been heard on our stage" (1971, 202)) but the critic André Levinson was less enthusiastic: "Tcherepnin's music, which was attractively orchestrated and quite sensitively adapted for dance, confines itself to only a few hints at eighteenth-century stylistic methods" (1982, 10). He voiced similar criticisms of the choreography: "Not reflecting the style of the epoch to any degree whatsoever (which could have served as the artistic justification of the dances), the dances in *Armide* are reduced to a broken series of episodes and details drawn from the arsenal of classical dance" (ibid.). Valerian Svetlov, who found the ballet's structure completely within the bounds of nineteenth-century style ("everything in its place"), none the less noted suggestions of future innovations in the work's choreography:

> The spirit of innovation is already in evidence here and there in the breaking and bending of tradition, the geometric rules of lines and structures, in the asymmetry of the group designs, in various darings, in various attempts to negate the academy, in various achievements. A kind of nerve of new inspiration pulses, some kind of new life beats.
>
> (1911, 3)

A film of Alexandra Danilova's 1979 staging of dances from *Armide* (for the School of American Ballet) substantiates Svetlov's view of the choreography: it closely resembles Petipa's choreography, save for an asymmetry evident even in the choreography of the variations. That asymmetry, like that of Gorsky in *Don Quixote*, became the distinguishing feature of the new ballet.

Unlike the Petipa–Vsevolozhsky *Ruses d'amour*, the most meticulously stylized of their series of eighteenth-century ballets, with its costumes and sets based on eighteenth-century models, and "genuine" heeled dancing shoes, *Armide* made no pretense of authenticity. The ballet's libretto was based on Gautier's romantic tale,[20] its score late romantic, its choreography employed the virtuoso dance technique of the last decades of the nineteenth century. *Armide*'s stylization represented a return to a nearer example: that of *Sleeping Beauty*. The stylization of the earlier work, primarily a function of the décor and theme, did not intrude upon or limit the choreography, music, or design. In this regard, *Armide* represents a revival of the nineteenth-century Russian, rather than eighteenth-century French ballet traditions.

Benois' writings on the ballet reveal that it is precisely this late nineteenth-century tradition he had hoped to revive. He had planned a full-length ballet, and his contributions to the resulting work show the same careful attention to period authenticity evident in the Petipa–Vsevolozhsky grand siècle works. But if *Armide* was meant to imitate *Sleeping Beauty* – the best of these – Benois' mixture of rococo and romantic and the need to abbreviate the work already signaled a departure from that tradition. *Sleeping Beauty* elevated a low genre, the *féerie*; the Benois–Fokine work effectively miniaturized the high-genre Petipa grand ballet.

Fokine began to experiment with romantic ballet themes in *Chopiniana*, his first version of *Les Sylphides*, produced months before the earliest version of *Armide*. *Sylphides* was the first in a series of Ballets Russes works set in the period of ballet romanticism and the one that most literally re-creates its period style. The export version of the ballet evolved into a romantic *ballet blanc*, complete with the familiar forest glade. The ballet has no plot: a *danseur noble* and three ballerinas in long white romantic-era tutus perform a series of variations to orchestrated Chopin piano works.

Sylphides is generally regarded as a milestone in the history of dance. "*Les Sylphides* is certainly the most poetical of ballets of the twentieth century and, perhaps, of all time" enthused Cyril Beaumont (1941, 567). Lyubov Blok, generally unsympathetic to Fokine's innovations, called the ballet a "turning point," the "pinnacle" (1987, 331). Like most historians, Blok views the work as the first plotless, non-narrative ballet.[21] But like so many of Fokine's "precedents," that distinction should be accorded his Moscow contemporary: Gorsky's staging of Glinka's *Valse fantaisie* (1901) anticipated Fokine's 1830s setting, his use of "romantic" long tutus, and his foray into "pure," plotless dance.

Sylphides re-created the era of romantic ballet, the age of *Giselle* and the original Sylphide, the period when point technique was still developing. Like *The Swan*, *Sylphides* effectively isolates the nineteenth-century ballet's white act, or vision scene, making it the ballet's subject while omitting any notion of plot. Fokine's ballerinas, possessed of the full range of techniques their Russian training afforded them, were asked not to use it: "Fokine, dismissing the 'steel toes' of his contemporary ballerinas, recreated the timid attempts of the danseuses of the 1830s to rise up on the tips of their toes in still-soft shoes and hold a difficult pose, if only for a second" (Krasovskaya 1971, 189). That choice amounted to a clear subordination of choreography to the ballet's stylization: the period style evoked by the décor, dance and music. What is more, the authenticity of the dance technique employed – as with any stylized technique in dance's "preliterate" (pre-video) period – was bound to be as unauthentic as any other. Fokine's sources were lithographs of Taglioni and other romantic ballerinas – his method of reconstructing the dances of the 1830s was not unlike Isadora's "recreation" of Greek dance, as Fokine admits in his memoirs: "I don't know if our dance ancestors danced this way – and no one else does either" (1981, 114).

As the first of the Fokine–Ballets Russes works to celebrate the ballet's romantic era, *Sylphides* signaled a departure from ballets like *Sleeping Beauty* or even *Le Pavillon d'Armide*. Those ballets paid homage to the eighteenth-century court ballet tradition (*Armide* referred as well to the summit of the nineteenth-century academy). *Les Sylphides* celebrates the romantic spirit, the period of the ballet's popular success before the bourgeois public of Paris' Grand Opera, and its liberation from the precepts of eighteenth-century neoclassicism. Ballet romanticism introduced new themes, a new focus on the female dancer, and an entirely new technique: dancing *en pointe*. Parallels to Fokine's era and his place in it abound. As the hegemony of the St Petersburg imperial ballet began to erode, popular, rather than aristocratic historical models inspired new ballets. Fokine's retrospectivism, focused as it was on romantic revolt, foreshadowed a new era of "public," popular ballet.

Sylphides' peculiar combination of innovation and false nostalgia – furthering the ballet's abstract expressive possibilities while scaling back its technique – offers a pointed example of the ballet's decadence in the Fokine (and Gorsky) period. *Sylphides* presented the romantic ballet in a new, abstract light, yet the subject had visibly faded. *Sleeping Beauty* and *Armide* were balletic backward glances, conscious evocations of privileged moments in dance history, but both used contemporary ballet technique, relying on music and décor to place the work chronologically. The choreography of *Sylphides*, like that of the most meticulously authenticized of Petipa's 1900 ballets, represents a conscious decision to authenticize historically – in other words, to diminish – the choreography as well. Where Aurora's madness in *Sleeping Beauty* could be indicated by subtle deformations of classical steps and *enchaînements*, and Armida's variation retained a crystalline classical purity, the reductive choreography of *Sylphides* signaled the new ballet's triumph of style over substance.

The new ballet's shift in focus – to story or stylization – could have only one result: the choreography quickly became less interesting. Indeed, the emphasis on décor in the Diaghilev ballet (and on plot in Gorsky's work) frequently rendered the choreography superfluous. Given the enormous popularity of the new ballet and the sheer volume of ballets produced (Garafola (1989) lists some eighty Fokine ballets choreographed from 1905 to 1917), the disappearance of the vast majority of these questions the accomplishment of their choreography.[22]

These ballets were products of their time, answering the symbolists' call for a dionysian theater with the farandoles that typically brought Fokine's works to a close. Unlike the proper, measured farandole in *Sleeping Beauty*'s hunt scene, Fokine's farandoles were writhing masses of humanity, orgiastic round-dance responses to symbolist "communality" in a theater that united performer and audience in dionysian ecstasy. Sergei Auslender's review of Fokine's choreography of the Polovtsian dances in *Prince Igor* implies a degree of success in breaking down the barriers of the "old" theater:

> Here is the finale, when all the lines of this severe design blend into one no less well-formed, a stream; overtaking, seizing, outrunning, struggling, one jumping across another – everyone . . . rushing the hall with a thunder, crashing the footlights, running in streams of complex figures, once again meeting and again, with more furious rejoicing, renewing their assault. If the curtain had been delayed for a second, it seemed that it couldn't have held and would have torn out into the hall, onto the square, the street, conquering and drawing everything with it.
>
> (1909, 30)

But the ballets of both Fokine and Gorsky became formulaic exercises almost from the start. In *On the Old and New Ballet* (1913a), a compilation of André Levinson's dance writings and reviews, Fokine's works are divided into "Eastern," "national," and "romantic" series. Most of Fokine's 1905–1917 work fits these categories as well. To *Schéhérazade* and *Cleopatra* of the Eastern series could be added *Les Orientales*, *Islamé*, and *Thamar*. *Papillons* and *Le Spectre de la rose* belong to Levinson's "romantic" category, with *Les Sylphides* and *Carnaval*. *Le Festin* and *Firebird*, Levinson's national series, were joined by the dances from the operas *Prince Igor*, *Sadko*, *Le Coq d'or*, and *Ruslan and Ludmila*, and the ballets *Petrushka* and *Stenka Razin*. Ballets on Greek and antique themes also comprised a significant portion of his 1905–1917 repertory: *Acis and Galatea*, *Eunice*, *Narcisse*, *Daphnis and Chloë*, *Eros*, and the dances for *Orpheus* and *Eurydice*.[23]

Gorsky's output, smaller than Fokine's, consisted primarily of the restaged ballets of other choreographers. Petipa had done his share of restagings while ballet master at the Maryinsky, but he typically augmented the old choreography with new scenes, like the *jardin animé* scene he appended to Mazilier's *Le Corsaire*. Gorsky effectively dismantled the old ballets, reconstructing them according to his understanding of the principles of the new theater. The most important of his original works cling to nineteenth-century precedents, with librettos adapted from novels, and narrative, rather than choreographic embellishments.

The two choreographers' use of music for dance remained the more problematic aspect of both men's work. In their desire to strengthen the dramatic content of ballet, both relegated music to a distinctly second place. For his part, Gorsky was content to rely on traditional "ballet music," distinguishable by its rhythmic and melodic suggestiveness. In his restagings of the old ballets, Gorsky typically reworked the narrative and the choreography and commissioned new sets and costumes, but retained the music from the old productions. The new music he chose could be as idiosyncratic as his use of Chopin piano music for Petronius' death scene, or the inclusion of Rubinstein in his production of *Le Corsaire*. While Fokine was careful to choose "serious" pre-existing music for his ballets and fortunate in the musical choices made for him in the Diaghilev ballet, Levinson found his treatment of the scores somewhat forced in the first case and frequently inadequate in the second. (Levinson reminded his readers that Petipa was able to choreograph masterpieces to "ballet" music (1911a, II, 23).)

Fokine produced his last works for the Diaghilev ballet in 1914. By that time, Gorsky's work also lacked the originality and force of his early original ballets and restagings. In his 1911 and 1913 articles on the new ballet, Levinson finds Fokine's and Gorsky's attempts to infuse classical dance with "meaning" and dramatically to motivate movement superfluous. To Levinson, Fokine's "archaeological" approach, which privileged ancient and Eastern dance forms over those from the Western tradition, represented the triumph of novelty over tradition, and the forms Fokine adopted for his ballets – especially the concluding farandole – became as predictable and tiresome as the formulas of the classical ballet.

Levinson's most serious charge concerned the erosion of classical dancing in Fokine's works: "Our current crisis in classical dance is a disease not new to the ballet; it repeats periodically; its unchanging symptom is the prevalence of pantomime" (1913a, 19). Even worse, the mime to which the dance was now subordinate trafficked in a kind of dionysian erotomania:

> The transformation of the stage into a huge boudoir is nothing but an unnecessary, ugly pleonasm, the destruction of the inner economy of the action. The vulgarized Dionysus of the "Bacchanalia" and the "Venus vulgivaga" of Fokine's erotic fantasies creep in as the ferment of the disintegration of the apollonian beauty of the "classical" ballet, whose banner might properly be the words of Nietzsche regarding the freeing of the soul from the oppression and strain of the dramatic experience through the fiction of ideal beauty: *Erlösung durch den Schein*.
>
> (1911a, II, 19)

Nietzsche (and Wagner) are invoked again in Levinson's discussion of the role of décor and music in the ballet theater. He sees the history of art as a process of differentiation of the various arts. Thus for Levinson, Wagner's theory of the total art work becomes "the primary disease of the contemporary theater. In my opinion . . . such a fusion, the realization of the *Gesamtkunstwerk* which combines in a single endeavor the potential of all the arts is possible only in their rudimentary stages" (1913a, 12). Levinson believed that one or more of the arts will naturally predominate when such a synthesis is attempted, but that in the new ballet, the dance had already ceded place to the visual arts and pantomime.

4

CRISIS IN THE ACADEMY:
THE DEATH
OF THE MAIDEN

T HE HISTORY of Russian ballet in the first years of the twentieth century – from Petipa's last works to the ballets of Gorsky, Fokine, and Nijinsky – is the story of the Russian dance academy in decline. But where Fokine and Gorsky tampered with academic formulas in their quest for dramatic truth and naturalistic stylization, Nijinsky launched a full-scale assault on the academy, a declaration of war. Levinson concluded his review of Nijinsky's first ballet, *L'Après-midi d'un faune* (1912), with a startling assessment of the new direction Diaghilev's Ballets Russes had chosen: "What is clear is that the fate of Diaghilev's ballet venture . . . is no longer tied to that of the Russian choreographic stage by any solid link" (1982, 62).

Of the four works Nijinsky choreographed for the Ballets Russes – *Faune*, *Jeux* (1912), *Le Sacre du printemps* (1913), and *Till Eulenspiegel* (1916) – only *Faune* has survived in the repertory. (The Joffrey Ballet mounted a reconstructed version of *Sacre* in 1987.) Still, few choreographers' works have attracted so much attention as Nijinsky's, whether in or out of the repertory. The 1980s witnessed the re-publication of Baron Adolf de Meyer's photographs of *Faune*, a *Faune* exhibition at the Musée d'Orsay in Paris, and a reconstruction of *Faune* from Nijinsky's notes. The reconstruction of *Sacre* in 1987 set off its own flurry of activity: premières, a conference devoted to the ballet, television programs, and scores of reviews, essays, and appreciations.

The greater share of the writing devoted to Nijinsky's ballets dwells on the choreographer's unorthodox movement vocabulary, ignoring the other half of the academic ballet equation: the choreographer's use of stage space. This discussion is unavoidable in the case of *Faune*, which was danced on a shallow stage. But works on *Sacre* – a ballet whose unorthodox spatial design is equally important, though less obvious – tend to ignore the issue entirely. These two interdependent functions should be examined together in order to gauge the full impact of Nijinsky's choreographic innovation. The staging of both ballets, like the movement vocabulary employed, counters the traditional staging of the Petipa ballet, negating the final stage in the evolution of the grand ballet on the perspective stage.[1]

L'Après-midi d'un faune

Discussions of Nijinsky's staging and his movement idioms invariably invoke Vsevolod Meyerhold's experimental stagings, especially those produced for the 1906–1907 season of Vera Kommissarzhevskaya's theater. But sources for Nijinsky's staging are plentiful and various. The static arrangement of performers horizontally on a narrow stage has its origins in *tableaux vivants*, never entirely absent from the ballet. A "living picture" depicting Apollo ended *Sleeping Beauty* and a similar tableau formed the first image of Fokine's *Animated Gobelins*.

Flattened stage perspectives and constrained movement were the stock in trade of Russian new theater; the design and use of the acting space played a key role in the evolution of new theater productions. The naturalistic stage design of the Duke of Meinigen's troupe provided a model for the productions of Stanislavsky's Art Theater. In turn, Meyerhold signaled an important departure from Art Theater practice in abandoning its meticulously scaled models of stage sets. His staging of Maeterlinck's *Death of Tintagiles* was the first of several experiments with the flattened stage perspective: *Hedda Gabler* was staged against a two-dimensional backdrop; photographs of the production of *Sister Beatrice* show actors in positions resembling friezes. The 1907 production of *Pelléas and Mélisande* was the last of these "flat" productions: Sologub's *Victory of Death* was staged with the actors placed forward on the proscenium, but "into a sculptural plane" in relation to the setting (Rudnitssky 1969, 124).[2] Meyerhold's 1907 production of Blok's *Balaganchik* suggests a primitivist source for these non-naturalistic stagings: the *"balagan*," the portable fairground booth that housed puppet shows.

The experimentation with stage space in the new, "conditional" theater represented an attempt to eliminate the traditional theater's barriers between performer and audience and to revive the communal theater of ancient Greece. A number of theoretical discussions and justifications of the new staging methods appeared in Russian theater and arts publications: Maeterlinck's "Contemporary Drama" appeared in *Mir iskusstva* in 1900, *Apollon* published George Fuchs' theory of the "relief" stage (1909–1910); his "Theater of the Twentieth Century" appeared in the 1911 *Ezhegodnik*. But the theoretical basis of the experimentation was less important to the dance theater than the promise this type of staging held in purely visual terms.

The foreshortening of the stage – groundbreaking and significant in the dramatic theater – represented a revolutionary rethinking of the staging of dance. Unlike the décor of the old ballet, which addressed the periphery of the stage, leaving a maximal amount of stage space for dancing, Bakst's shallow set severely limited the type of movement that could be employed. The choreography, planned with new limitations in mind, avoided classical technique entirely, substituting a flattened, angular movement that adopted the poses of Greek vases so literally that stasis, rather than movement, became the production's salient feature.

Mayer believes that Bakst suggested the two-dimensional staging to Nijinsky "as a way to solve the problem of recreating in three-dimensional space the rhythms of the flat, painted figures found on the sides of Greek vases" (1977, 139). This method of stylization signaled a radical departure from Isadora's and Fokine's renderings of ancient Greek dance in its move away from the free "hellenistic" movement Nijinsky's predecessors represented as Greek (what Levinson called the "simplified and vulgarized hellenism of our day" (1982, 26)).

Nijinsky's movement vocabulary was not without precedent. Yakovlev maintains that Petipa turned to Egyptian art when choreographing *Daughter of the Pharaoh* (1862): "in order more accurately to recreate archae-ologically the sculptural contours of the unique Egyptian style" (1924, 25). Fokine claims to have choreographed his dance for the three Egyptian girls in *Eunice* (1907) in profile and used the style again in *Une Nuit d'Egypte* (1908) (1981, 95). But Nijinsky's ballet marked the first use of these poses to sustain an entire ballet, elevating them from affectation to idiom in much the same way that Fokine freed the divertissement in *Les Sylphides*, making it the subject of his ballet. In isolating a style of movement previously used for character dancing or effect, Nijinsky developed a complete vocabulary of steps and gestures for use in only one ballet, carrying Fokine's principle of the appropriateness of movement to the work's genre to its logical extreme. The result, neither more nor less "authentic" than Fokine's or Petipa's stylized treatments of "ancient" movement, represented a compelling investigation of the possibilities of movement for its own sake.

The Ballets Russes audience, expecting the unexpected from Diaghilev's ballet, responded appropriately to the work's sexual impropriety (Nijinsky simulated masturbation) and the novelty of the collaborators' idiomatic rethinking of ancient stylization. Yet the novelty of *Faune* and the scandal surrounding the concluding auto-erotic gesture masked the truly radical implications of the ballet's choreography and staging. For four seasons the Diaghilev ballet had altered the public perception of ballet, successfully challenging grand ballet traditions. With *Faune* that challenge extended to the stage space and to the movement itself.

The poet, philosopher, and sometime dance critic Nikolai Minsky's review "A Startling Ballet," best summarizes the true import of the ballet's stylization: "Apollo cedes place to Dionysus, and the curtain falls" (*Utro rossii*, 24 May 1912).

Le Sacre du printemps

Although Nijinsky's next ballet, *Le Sacre du printemps*, developed the experiments with space and movement begun with *Faune*, Nijinsky did not return to the "flat" stage. But *Sacre* would not want for novelty. Perhaps more than any other ballet in the history of dance, *Sacre* has been saddled with an astonishing array of symbolic meanings. The notion of apocalypse, both social and cultural is the most far-reaching of these, and the first to be realized, as the First World War began the following year. Nijinsky's madness, highly romanticized in the literature and lore of dance, is another. The First World War has come to symbolize the definitive end of nineteenth-century European culture and mores; the ballet holds a similar place for those who would ascribe a date to the emergence of modernism. Modris Eksteins, whose book *Rites of Spring: The Great War and the Birth of the Modern Age* uses the ballet's "orgiastic-nihilistic irony" as its principal motif, calls *Sacre* "a landmark of modernism" (xiv). Garafola writes that "the ballet has become synonymous with the very idea of modernity" (1989, 51).

Leaving aside the cultural-historical significance of the ballet, the scandal surrounding its première, and even the controversy regarding its current reconstruction, it remains to examine *Sacre* as a ballet – and a ballet in the Russian tradition. In that context, Nijinsky's *Sacre* reveals itself as the definitive anti-ballet, a work which makes a point of reviling every notion the classical ballet held dear. Its music, choreography, and staging all challenge the authority of a centuries-old lyric theater tradition.

Sacre was the brainchild of Igor Stravinsky (1882–1971), who envisioned a ballet based on a pagan rite culminating in the sacrifice of a virgin. His collaborator was Nikolai Roerich (1874–1947), the painter and scholar of ancient Russia, who had designed Borodin's *Prince Igor* and Rimsky-Korsakov's *Ivan the Terrible* for Diaghilev's 1909 season. Their collaboration resulted in a ballet that, like *Faune*, could not be "authentic" in any historical or anthropological sense, but remained true to its own method of stylization, a seamless entity without the juxtaposition of classical and non-classical dancing that disturbed even Fokine's work.

Several writers, Garafola among them, point out that "neither ancient tale nor Slavonic lore offers a precedent for female sacrifice" (1989, 72). Other writers have discussed Aztec rites, Sergei Gorodetsky's Yarilo poems, and works of Velimir Khlebnikov and Alexei Remizov as possible sources (ibid., 426–427, n. 58). Of course, the source for the ballet's female sacrifice was much closer at hand. The nineteenth-century ballet repertory offered a number of well-known precedents, from Giselle and the sylphide to the bayadère and Aurora. Like Vsevolozhsky, Stravinsky and Roerich turned to the romantic ballet's basic plot for the structure of their first ballet libretto.

In Stravinsky's sketch of the libretto, included in a letter to Nikolai Findeizen, the critic and authority on early Russian music, the procession of the village elder interrupts the games that open the ballet. At the climax of the first scene the elder kisses the earth. The second scene depicts the "secret night games" of the village maidens. One is condemned to be sacrificed, and, like the victims of the wilis wrath, is forced to dance herself to death as the elders watch (V. Stravinsky and Craft 1979, 82).

Although Stravinsky's ballet is in one act, its structure is dual (like *Giselle*), contrasting the daytime games of village youths with the mysterious nocturnal rites of the maidens. The naïve activities of the first act become spiritually and mystically charged in the second, preserving the essential romantic duality of the material and spirit worlds. An interview with Roerich reveals a further correspondence to *Giselle*: "The action begins on a summer night and ends before the sunrise when the first rays are seen" (1971, 429): the ritual murder must be accomplished before the dawn, echoing the romantic opposition of day and night, material and spirit worlds.

While retaining this basic duality, the librettists shift the ballet's "mad" scene, the sacrifice, from its usual position at the end of the first narrative sequence to the end of the ballet. The ballet retains a *ballet blanc* of sorts – the maidens' dances comprise most of the second scene – but without the traditional *raisons d'être*. In transferring the mad scene from the first to the final scene, the librettists make it the ballet's choreographic and narrative climax. Where the mad scene had once occasioned another scene, the maiden's dance in *Sacre* (the ballet's only solo) serves as the work's dénouement. Fokine's *Dying Swan* depicted the death of a nineteenth-century ballet icon. *Sacre* does away with the old ballet's chief protagonist – the village maiden – while the village watches.

Taken individually, the components of *Sacre* would not portend the controversy surrounding the ballet's first performances. Death had functioned almost as an organizing principle in Fokine's harem orgies, and depictions of ancient *Rus'* were familiar and admired in Paris. But where Stravinsky's *Firebird* and *Petrushka* were poeticized representations of ancient and modern Russia, designed by the veteran stage designers Golovin and Benois, Roerich based his designs for *Sacre* on his archaeologist's knowledge of pre-literate Slavic cultures, rather than theatrical practice.[3] The juxtaposition of Stravinsky's and Nijinsky's comparatively radical statements with Roerich's museum-like, naturalistic décor results in the work's basic tension, its confluence of the two main lines of Russian new ballet: Moscow naturalism and Petersburg stylization; Gorsky's exceedingly literal stagings of narrative ballets versus Fokine's elaborate costume dramas.

Richard Taruskin sees a "downright subversion" of mainstream composition in Stravinsky's score. For Taruskin, Stravinsky's sketchbook for *Sacre* reveals the "*abstraction of stylistic elements from folk music* that marked such a turning point in Stravinsky's development as a composer" (1982, 79). This subversion of the mainstream, the academy, is the goal of Nijinsky's choreography as well. And the movement style developed for the work contradicts the basic tenets of academic dance: the struggle to overcome gravity and exaggerate the length of the body's lines.

The photographs that survive from the original production of *Sacre* show dancers in contorted poses, with turned-in bent knees, angular arms, and contracted torsos – the kind of non-balletic poses that elicited cries for doctors and dentists from dissatisfied members of the first-night audience. The critic André Levinson noted a similar tension in the movement: "A kind of all-powerful irresistible constraint rules over them, twisting their limbs, pressing down on bowed necks. It seems that any other movement, more free or harmonious, is forbidden them, would be blasphemous" (1913–1914, 34). Nijinsky replaced the graceful movement of the old ballet with stamping motions, shaking and trembling. The pull of gravity is evident. The maiden is chosen because she falls, overwhelmed by the pull of the earth.

Nijinsky's new movement idiom was not without precedent. Turned-in, stooped dancing, the antithesis of the ballet's lofty verticality, connoted evil in the old ballet. Carabosse's pages in *Sleeping Beauty* furnish a prime example of the ballet's equation of physical distortion and loathsomeness.[4] Krasovskaya suggests another precedent for this type of movement. The actor and playwright S. I. Antimonov recalled that in the 1900 MKhAT production of Ostrovsky's *Snowmaiden*, the actors moved "with feet turned in . . . the way the ancient Slavs walked" (1971, 434).

Sacre's unconventional movement vocabulary represents the culmination of an assault on the classical dance academy begun with *Faune*. Nijinsky's treatment of stage space, a modish affectation in *Faune*, represents an outright reappraisal of the traditional use of the perspective stage in *Sacre* – a primary determinant in the development of the modern *danse d'école*.

Several groups of dancers are on-stage at the beginning of Millicent Hodson's reconstruction of *Sacre*. The dancers in each group form a rough circle; the placement of the groups on the stage appears random. Even from an ideal vantage point (the center of the balcony in a theater where the stage is not raked) some groups are obscured by others. What is more, the groups face inward, away from the audience. The haphazard arrangement of the groups, and turn away from the audience are typical of the stage pictures Nijinsky uses throughout the ballet. The Chosen Maiden's dance – performed center-stage, facing the audience – is the sole exception to the ballet's general rule of ignoring the public. One critic wrote: "At times it seemed as though the choreographer was not concerned about the audience's seeing everything" (Horwitz 1987, 68). The meaning of the audience's exclusion from the action on-stage is clear. In the words of another critic, "repeatedly, Nijinsky flanked the front of the stage with dancers. He was unafraid to exclude the audience from what takes place. This is a private ritual; we, sealed off, peek apprehensively between their legs" (Anawalt 1987, 72). Volkonsky offered a terse analysis of the work's first performances: "*Le Sacre du printemps* isn't a 'ballet.' It is a ritual, an ancient ceremonial rite. Nothing could be less appropriate to prepare one for this spectacle than the word 'ballet' and all the associations it carries with it" (1913, 72). André Levinson wrote: "The laws of scenic reality are hardly the same as the particulars of primitive ethnography; our brave searchers of innovation repeated their usual mistake of theatrical naturalism – now obsolete" (1913–1914, 34–35).

Nijinsky's non-traditional use of stage space conveys the ritual nature of the performance; it also continues a line of choreographic innovation begun with *Faune*. The raked perspective stage was the primary determinant in the development of the vocabulary of classical ballet. The poses, movements, placement, and scale of classical dance assume this traditional setting. In denying the validity of this convention, Nijinsky disregards not only the principles of turn-out, verticality, and virtuosity, but the governing principle which had led to their development. In doing so, he effectively choreographed the academy's demise and forced the experiments of the new ballet to their logical end. But in inventing an entirely new movement vocabulary for his ballets – an idea generally attributed to Fokine – Nijinsky went much further than his predecessor, renouncing the academy's movement tradition, the basis of his own virtuosity and his interpreters' training. With *Sacre* Nijinsky explored the limits of ballet naturalism, incorporating ritual design and chance elements into a movement style that anticipated dance expressionism.

Critical and historical works on Russian ballet tend to regard Nijinsky's choreography – especially that of *Sacre* – as a kind of anomaly. Western observers of these ballets were generally ill-equipped to evaluate their place in the history of Russian dance, with which they were mostly unfamiliar. This unfamiliarity with the canon and tradition of Russian academic dance has plagued studies of the Diaghilev era in dance history more than any other, as Soviet scholars have likewise been unable or unwilling to discuss these works in the proper context of Russian modernism. Vera Krasovskaya's conflation of Russian new ballet and the aesthetics of Petersburg's acmeist poets is a particularly puzzling example:

Acmeism arose already in the 1910s as a negation of the poetics of symbolism, and elements of its aesthetic were soon evident in the Paris productions of the Russian ballet. The earthy basis for feelings, the interest in the "tangible world" and "beautiful clarity" of forms announced themselves in such productions as Mikhail Fokine's *Polovtsian Dances* and *Schéhérazade*, and most importantly, in the works of the great dancer Vatslav Nijinsky. The images of the heroes created by Nijinsky in the ballets of Fokine – those of the "first man's" perceptions of the world – brought to life one of the primary themes of acmeist poetry.

(1971, 9)

It would be difficult to imagine two aesthetics more diametrically opposed than that of Fokine and the acmeist poets, whose impact will be discussed in the following chapters. While Krasovskaya's comparison is chronologically sound, it is practically untenable. The mad dionysian whirl of Fokine's dance for the Polovtsy and the harem massacre that drenches *Schéhérazade* in blood share nothing with the beautiful clarity that the poet Mikhail Kuzmin championed, or the lapidary quality of acmeist verse. As for the roles Nijinsky created in Fokine's works, the most famous – a slave, a rose, and a puppet – dehumanized and emasculated him.

In truth, the Ballets Russes aesthetic was closely linked to that of the Russian symbolists, and the ballet's inherent synaesthesia assured the medium's suitability as a venue for symbolist art. The new ballet's favorite themes – drawn from the commedia dell'arte and romanticized retrospectivism, depicting legends of ancient *Rus'*, carnivals, and intoxication by a rose – meshed with those of the symbolist poets. And correspondences between the Diaghilev repertory and literary symbolism were not lost on contemporary critics: Turgendkhold compared Fokine's *Carnaval* to Blok's play *Balaganchik* [*The Fairground Booth*] in a 1910 review in *Apollon* (1910a, 69); Kostylev discussed the otherworldliness of Ballets Russes scenic design (1910, 29). Even the "crisis" of literary symbolism in 1910 had its balletic parallel in the Fokine/Diaghilev split in 1912 and in the cataclysm surrounding Nijinsky's 1912 and 1913 ballets.

The parallels between the culture of symbolism and the Diaghilev ballet extend to two works which effectively mark the end of their respective movements: Nijinsky's *Sacre* and Andrei Bely's novel *Petersburg*. Bely began working on his novel in 1911, one year after Stravinsky had begun *Sacre*, and both works appeared in 1913 (Bely's work was serialized in the journal *Sirin*, 1913–1914). In Bely's novel, Apollon Apollonovich, the lover of symmetry and order, represents official imperial Petersburg. Apollon's dionysian son, Nikolai, a bomb-toting, would-be patricide, inhabits a different Petersburg, a motley collection of islands teeming with undesirable inhabitants. The novel juxtaposes apollonian Occidental order and dionysian Oriental anarchy with an urgency symbolized by the ticking bomb Nikolai carries.

Sacre is pregnant with similar tensions, employing the trappings of the ballet, the quintessential apollonian art form, to depict a chaotic, barbaric ritual. Self-destruction – the dionysian overthrow of that order – is immanent in both works. And both employ standard nineteenth-century genres – the novel, the grand ballet – as vehicles for the subversion of their respective academies. In both examples, the aura of apocalypse is achieved through a careful manipulation of language. In Bely's novel, chapters, sentences, and even words are broken and deformed, frustrating the acts of reading and interpretation. Nijinsky's language is a similarly inchoate rendering of the nineteenth-century dance vocabulary. The death of the maiden, Nijinsky's ticking bomb, effectively deals the death blow to the nineteenth-century academic ballet.

In her book *Sexual Personae*, a study of art and decadence in the Western tradition, Camille Paglia maintains that "the Dionysian is no picnic. It is the chthonian realities which Apollo evades, the blind grinding of subterranean force, the long slow suck, the murk and ooze" (1990, 5–6). The shock of the new, for *Sacre*'s audiences, was the new ballet's inherent dionysianism, now carried to its logical extreme and unmasked. The music critic Boris Asafyev (who published under the pseudonym Igor Glebov) wrote: "There is nothing in common with our notions of ancient dionysian orgies here, nor could there be: this . . . is a heavy, sedentary mass that doesn't even attempt to tear itself from the earth – it longs to root itself in it, to fuse with it" (1929, 57). Where Fokine's ballets carefully maintained a patina of "art," Nijinsky did away with pretense. Reviewing the first performances of *Sacre*, Jacques Rivière wrote: "This is not a 'work of art' with all the usual little contrivances. Nothing is blurred, nothing obscured by shadows; there is no veiling or poetic mellowing, no trace of aesthetic effect" (1983, 115).

The ballet's disappearance from the repertory (after nine performances) demonstrated the paradox of "dionysian" ballet. Paglia defines the dionysian in art as "the *new*, exhilarating but rude, sweeping all away to begin again." Whereas "Apollo is law, history, tradition, the dignity and safety of custom and form" (Paglia 1990, 97). Fokine's ballets responded to the first half of Paglia's formulation, but clung to apollonian dignity and safety. Nijinsky's *Sacre* exchanged these pretensions for rudeness and the privilege of sweeping away tradition.

Yet in doing so, the ballet could satisfy no public. Where *Faune* had outraged and titillated, *Sacre* merely outraged. Diaghilev's audience, cultivated by Fokine's false dionysianism, beat a hasty retreat to custom and form. For *Sacre*'s Russian critics, whose understanding of ballet was based on Petipa's academicisms, rather than Fokine's reforms, Nijinsky's ballet was merely a puzzle. One senses exasperation in Levinson's review of the work: he finds both the libretto and score structureless, the choreography without artistic rationale (1982, 52–55).

That the type of movement Nijinsky pioneered in *Sacre* – weighted and coarse, contracted and unlovely – would find its place in twentieth-century "modern" dance only supports this theory of dance decadence. Modern dance began as a protest against the classical ballet. In Nijinsky's work one sees a similar protest, already fully formed.

5

TWO
APOLLOS

A S THE curtain rises on George Balanchine's *Apollo* (titled *Apollon Musagète* at its 1928 première), the eponymous god stands center-stage in profile, his right arm extended above and behind him, the left holding a long-necked lute that rests on his hip (Illustration 1). Apollo's right, extended arm begins to swing in large circles, strumming the lute. The gesture is autoerotic, though its implications have gone politely undiscussed in the criticism. With his flattened pose and unseemly gesture, Balanchine's Apollo begins where Nijinsky's Faun left off: the supremely dionysian act that concluded Nijinsky's work is a point of departure for Balanchine, whose choreography conveys in one terse gesture the "wild, half-human" quality of the youth who will acquire "nobility through art" (Balanchine and Mason 1977, 26).

Balanchine's *Apollo* is one of two Apollos to be discussed in this chapter. The other is *Apollon*, a journal published in St Petersburg from 1909 to 1917. Both the ballet and the journal are the progeny of Mir iskusstva, the Diaghilev-led organization that produced the journal and art exhibitions under that name. The ballet was one of the last produced by Diaghilev's Ballets Russes; the journal was based on the *Mir iskusstva* model, and featured the work of many of its former contributors. The two Apollos represent a second stage in the development of Mir iskusstva's world of art:

a reasoned response to the frankly dionysian aesthetic of the symbolists and decadents who shaped Russian arts and letters in the first decade of the new century.

This apollonian return to the certainty of form would manifest itself in several key areas of Russian artistic culture. It would temper the chaotic intensity of symbolist literature, painting, and music; impose a new order upon architecture's *style moderne*; and return choreography to a central place in ballet composition. The revival of arts academies attended this return to form. In the case of literature, where formal academies did not exist, they were invented. In dance, where the Petipa academy remained largely intact, the academy was revived in a more modern guise.

The two Apollos heralded a second, transitional phase of Russian modernism as the retrospective stylization that characterized Mir iskusstva-era visual art and dance gave way to serious formal investigations of past art, once plundered primarily for ornamental detail. The art of the past came to provide stylistic models rather than models for stylization in this period, and the new interest in the past resulted in scholarly investigations into the origins and histories of Russian arts and letters. Music and dance, painting and poetry existed in Russia long before Peter the Great's program of Westernization and secularization. But the eighteenth century represented a momentous new beginning for the arts in Russia. For the first time, imperial patronage supported large-scale imitation and adaptation of Western, secular forms.

The new-found recognition of and respect for the eighteenth-century origins of these Russian arts traditions characterize several branches of the fine and performing arts in Russia on the eve of the twentieth century, and mark an important transition from Mir iskusstva retrospectivism to "Apollon-ian" classicism. In the 1910s and 1920s, Russia's eighteenth-century attempts to assimilate Western art became classics in their own right. The resulting "discovery" of national arts traditions furnished this second phase of Russian modernism with its own set of "classical" antecedents. Each of these tendencies – the shift from retrospectivism to a new kind of classicism, the increasing professionalization of those involved in the industry of art, and the new regard for local arts traditions – distinguished the art of this second phase of Russian modernism from its first.

The scholarship that characterized the work of *Apollon*'s contributors, and the new regard for Russia's own high art traditions (a reassessment of both Russian and Western classical patrimonies), reflected the main lines of Petersburg's inherently conservative artistic culture of the 1910s and 1920s.

81

Like the ballet of the same name, the journal *Apollon* and the writings –
both creative and critical – that appeared in it represent a final stage in the
evolution of Russian retrospectivism, to the extent that it may properly be
called twentieth-century classicism.

Beyond Mir iskusstva:
Apollon and classical revival

Mir iskusstva ceased publication in 1904. Its immediate successors, *Vesy*
[*Libra*] and *Zolotoe runo* [*The Golden Fleece*], featured many of the Diaghilev
journal's contributors, but lacked its vision and scope. The two Moscow
journals patterned themselves after *Mir iskusstva*, reporting on Russian and
European visual art as well as literature. But the factional fighting that led
to the demise of the symbolist movement also contributed to the cessation
of both journals in 1909. Not until the founding of *Apollon* (also in 1909)
did a Russian journal equal *Mir iskusstva* in importance for the Russian
modernist movement as a whole.

Like *Mir iskusstva*, *Apollon* focused on literature and visual arts, although the
collaborators of both journals concerned themselves with the broad spectrum
of Russian art activity.[1] Both were products of St Petersburg's artistic milieu,
though Moscow artists contributed to each. Both were designed by leading
graphic artists (Bakst and Dobuzhinsky were among those chiefly responsible
for the look of the two journals). But for all their similarities, the two journals
represent two very different phases of Russian modernism, and their
dissimilarities point to the rapid change in Russian art in the relatively short
period of time from *Mir iskusstva*'s demise to *Apollon*'s founding. *Mir iskusstva*'s
pioneering forays into the history and origins of the Russian arts at the turn of
the century were echoed by full-fledged scholarly inquiries and studies on the
pages of *Apollon* a decade later. The stylization that typified Mir iskusstva's
retrospectivist tributes (Benois' depictions of Versailles, the Fokine–Benois
Pavillon d'Armide) ceded place to works that revealed a new "professional"
interest in "classical" notions of form in the Russian arts.

Several charter members of the Mir iskusstva group contributed to
Apollon,[2] but their contributions affirmed their allegiances to the new
aesthetic. Benois introduced the journal with the essay "In Expectation of a
Hymn to Apollo." Bakst's "The Paths of Classicism in Art" appeared in the
following two issues. As *Apollon*'s editor, Sergei Makovsky, noted, the name

alone announced a break with the old aesthetic: "Apollon. In the very title is the path we've chosen" (1909, 3).

Makovsky declared the journal's program to "assert rather than destroy norms" (Mickiewicz 1975, 368) in the first issue and identified the journal's "battle plan," which recognized "the necessity of guarding our cultural heritage in the name of the future" (ibid., 4). The editor recommended the lesson of past art as a solution to the current morass of formless art. None the less, his classicism looks to the future:

> This is, least of all, a newly-recovered path to the debts of ancient art. If classicism (the imitation of the perfection of the artists of Greece and the Renaissance) is once again possible, then only as a momentary enthusiasm or as a protest against the formless daring of work that has forgotten the laws of cultural continuity. Certainly, this protest is being felt now in literature and in the visual arts. It is possible that it is destined to express itself more clearly, formally.
>
> (ibid., 3)

Apollon's "world of art" was larger and more inclusive than that of *Mir iskusstva*. *Apollon*'s first issue featured essays on music, theater, poetry, architecture, and painting. The second included articles on the Munich Art Theater, Musorgsky's *Salammbô*, and Bakst's seminal essay "The Paths of Classicism in Art," in which the artist foresaw a new classicism in the visual arts and a return to the human figure in painting. Dance enjoyed an unprecedented prominence in *Apollon*. Where *Mir iskusstva* limited dance-writing to reviews, *Apollon* included historical and theoretical essays.

The activities of the "Apollonians," especially the journal's literary wing, furnish a comprehensive example of the new tendencies making themselves felt in Petersburg art of the 1910s and 1920s. Writers' circles had always played a role in the Russian literary world, but the associations founded by the second generation of modernist poets resembled formal academies of literature rather than the friendly circles of an earlier time. The writers who organized around *Apollon* in March 1909 called their group the Academy of Verse [Akademiya stikha]. In his article "*Apollo* and Modernist Poetics," Denis Mickiewicz summarizes the purposes of their meetings:

> To present and discuss unpublished fiction of special thematic or method-ological interest, to demonstrate "discoveries" in the history or theory of poetry, and (since the "society" boasted among its members such a number of prominent classical philologists) to read and discuss recent translations and original stylizations of classical sources.
>
> (ibid., 367)

The Poet's Guild [Cekh poetov], a second poetic "academy" founded in 1911 by Nikolai Gumilyov and Sergei Gorodetsky, also included a number of poets affiliated with *Apollon*. The group's name recalled medieval trade guilds and emphasized the organizers' belief in the role of literary craftsmanship. This backward glance represented something quite different from the retrospectivism of the previous decades – it referred to artistic production, rather than the product. The art of the past provided these poets with models for emulation rather than fodder for popularized classical stylizations, and the models they chose expanded the "canon" of classics beyond familiar ancient Greek or neoclassical French sources. Their writings demonstrate a familiarity with the variety of world literature, past and present. They produced scholarly studies of Pushkin and essays on Chenièr and Villon. Gumilyov's own models included Homer, Dante, Shakespeare, Rabelais, Villon, Gautier, and Wilde, as well as Pushkin and Lermontov.

The work of Innokenty Annensky – poet, playwright, critic, and philologist – provides an example of the increasing erudition of creative artists. Between 1901 and 1906, Annensky wrote three original tragedies based on Greek themes. His translations of Euripides began to appear in 1907. This shift, from stylization to scholarship, reflects a general pattern of Petersburg art of this period: as poets were more likely philologists than *amateurs* and poetic stylization gave way to literary artifact, the scholarly bent of *Apollon* supplanted the dilettantism of *Mir iskusstva*.[3]

Reclaiming Russia's classical patrimony

The apollonians' admiration for academies found an unlikely echo in a speech Alexandre Benois delivered to the All-Russian Congress of Artists in 1912. "Much that is new has accumulated and has not been brought into order, into a system," Benois cautioned, suggesting that the academy, with its authority and resources, might best cope with these difficulties (quoted in Kennedy 1977, 47–48). Janet Kennedy notes that although Benois wished to rejuvenate the academy, "in many respects . . . Benois envisaged simply a return of the institution to its original ideals and functions – creation of a monumental art for public places and the teaching of art as a 'system of inherited skills and knowledge'" (ibid.).

In the early years of Mir iskusstva, Benois, Diaghilev, and their associates had virtually defined their movement vis-à-vis the arts academy (see ibid.,

38–48). Benois' surprising advocacy of the academy in 1912 suggests a substantive reappraisal of his view of the institution – a re-evaluation that helps to explain the presence of so many *miriskussniki* on *Apollon*'s masthead. As the Mir iskusstva movement began to ebb (*c.* 1903), Benois' career – as artist and art historian – reflected the transition to the new apollonian aesthetic of Russian modernism's middle period, and testifies to the pivotal role Benois continued to play in Petersburg's artistic circles in the first decades of the twentieth century.

Benois' most conspicuous contribution to the second wave of Russian modernism remained his insistent advocacy of the art of the past, an advocacy that assumed many guises. But by the early 1900s, the focus of much of Benois' retrospectivism had shifted from French to Russian art. He began a series of paintings of Petersburg's eighteenth-century palaces in 1900, echoing an earlier (1897–1898) group of paintings depicting Versailles in the time of Louis XIV. After 1900, Benois wrote extensively on the history of Russian art, often focusing on art and life in the eighteenth century. He anticipated Petersburg's bicentennial in 1903 with a series of articles in *Mir iskusstva* ("Painterly Petersburg," "The Architecture of Petersburg," and "The Beauty of Petersburg"), authored polemical pieces in defense of Petersburg's architectural heritage ("Material for a History of Vandalism in Russia: The Destruction of the Mikhailovsky Palace"), and numerous studies on the history of Russian art. Although Benois' erudition and talent made him unique even in Mir iskusstva's rarefied circle, his turn to a specifically Russian retrospectivism (especially his reappraisal of Petersburg),[4] and the scholarly fervor with which he approached his subject fuse the most general tendencies of this second phase of Russian modernism.

Writing history

Benois was hardly alone in his quest to reclaim Russia's artistic heritage. The period from 1890–1910 witnessed the compilation of a number of histories of the Russian arts, most notably in dance and the visual arts. The *Ezhegodnik*, published in St Petersburg from 1892–1915, furnishes an early example of this trend. Created as part of Vsevolozhsky's reform of the state theaters, the annual chronicled the history of the Russian stage (including drama, music, and dance) from its first issues, in addition to providing information regarding the day-to-day administration of the theaters, their

casting, repertory, and personnel. The index to the first twelve volumes lists
a surprising variety of articles pertaining to the history of theater in Russia:

"The Court Ballet in Russian from its Origins to the Reign of Emperor
Aleksandr I," "An Essay on Ancient Choreography," "The History of
Theatrical Spectacles and Public Entertainments in Russia," "A Short Essay on
the Organization of the Administration of the Imperial Theaters in the Reign
of Emperor Aleksandr I," "Amateur Theater under Catherine II," "Amateur
Theater under Anna Ivanova," "Trivia of the Old Theater," "The Moscow
Theater in the Good Old Days," "At the Home of the Russian Theater,"
"Russian Opera in the Eighteenth Century," "The Celebration in Peterhof on
the Occasion of the Wedding of Kseniya Aleksandrovna to Mikhail
Aleksandrovich," "Russian Theater under Peter the Great," "Verses of the
Skomorokhi in Eighteenth-Century Manuscripts," "Sumarokov as a
Dramaturg," "Ancient Choreography."[5]

Dance and the visual arts show evidence of the most assiduous
assimilation of their histories at the turn of the century. Several of
Petersburg's balletomanes/critics wrote histories and pseudo-historical
reminiscences of the Russian ballet in the 1890s. Aleksandr Pleshcheev's *Our
Ballet* (1896), the first history of Russian ballet, covers all dance activity in
Russia through the eighteenth century, and focuses on the Petersburg ballet
in the nineteenth. Konstantin Skalkovsky's *In the Theater World* (1899) is a
theatergoer's memoir with an extensive section devoted to Russian ballet in
the 1880s and 1890s.[6]

Like *Apollon*'s contributors, anxious to expand the canon beyond the
obvious and the familiar, later scholars attempted to chronicle the broader
range of dance history, including eighteenth-century court ballet, the dance
of ancient Greece, and non-Western dance forms. André Levinson admired
Maurice Emmanuel's *La Danse grecque antique*, published in Paris in 1896,
and cited the work repeatedly in his essay "On the Old and New Ballet,"
published in the *Ezhegodnik* in 1913. Levinson also wrote on eighteenth-
century dance: "Noverre and the Aesthetics of Ballet in the Eighteenth
Century" appeared in *Apollon* in 1912. Valerian Svetlov, like Levinson, wrote
on both ancient Greek choreography and early Russian ballet (including the
Ezhegodnik article on court ballet in Russia cited in the list above). Several
writers' works purport to cover the entire history of dance. Nikolai
Vashkevich's *The History of Dances of All Times and Peoples* (the first and
only volume of which was published in 1908) comprised three sections:
"The Ancient East," "Antiquity," and "The Art of Duncan." Sergei
Khudekov's three-volume work, *The History of Dances*, appeared in

1913–1918. Writing in *Apollon* E. A. Stark summarized: "The Russian ballet thundered over the whole world. What is more, the Russian ballet gave birth to an entire literature about itself" (1915, 65).

Benois' works comprised a sizable portion of the histories of the Russian visual arts that appeared in Russia in the first years of the new century: *The History of Painting in the Nineteenth Century, Russian Painting* (1901), *The Russian School of Painting* (1904), and the all-encompassing *The History of Painting of All Times and Peoples* (1912–17), whose title echoes Vashkevich's. Benois also edited the journal *Khudozhestvennoe sokrovishche Rossii* [The Art Treasures of Russia] from 1901 to 1903, and contributed to *Starye gody* [Bygone Years] a journal of art and antiquities. Another former *miriskussnik*, Igor Grabar, published the first volume of his monumental *History of Russian Art* in 1909.

Diaghilev authored a monograph on the eighteenth-century painter Dmitry Levitskii in 1902, but his greatest contribution to the history of Russian art remains the 1905 exhibition of Russian historical portraits. Diaghilev traveled throughout Russia (and in Europe) for several years, gathering nearly three thousand portraits for the exhibition. His achievement ranks with that of any historian in its quite literal assemblage and revelation of a crucial, though largely forgotten stage in the development of Russian painting.

Petersburg classicism

Mark Etkind discusses Benois' work at the turn of the century as a campaign to rehabilitate "artistic Petersburg" (1989, 79). The tone of the concluding lines of "Painterly Petersburg" confirms Etkind's assertion and indicates the central place the historical city occupied in Benois' retrospectivist program:

> One wished that artists loved Petersburg, and, consecrating and promoting its beauty, would themselves save it from ruin, stopping its barbaric distortion, defending its beauty from the encroachment of rude ignoramuses, treating them with such unbelievable scorn so that all the sooner one might find only voices of protest, voices of protection, voices of enthusiasm.
>
> (ibid., 5)

Benois' campaign represents an attempt to restore the reputation of a city long vilified in nineteenth-century literature. Karamzin's Petersburg was built on a swamp of "tears and corpses"; Pushkin's city perches precipitously at the boundary of chaos and deluge; Gogol and Dostoevsky cast the city as an exemplar of artificiality, a source of estrangement and modern alienation. In the literary tradition, monumental, bureaucratic, European Petersburg represented the antithesis of holy, organic, Russian Moscow — the modern rational city versus the ancient historical one.

The success of Benois' campaign may be judged by the astonishing array of *Mir irkusstva* tributes to the imperial city and its suburbs in the years following its bicentennial. Mir iskusstva artists had always flirted with retrospectivism, but the paintings of this second phase engage Russian imperial history more specifically and frequently than was previously the case. Some of these addressed historical themes, such as Evgeny Lanceray's *Petersburg at the Beginning of the Eighteenth Century* (1906), or Benois' *Parade in the Reign of Paul I* (1907) and *The Appearance of Catherine II at Tsarskoe Selo* (1909). Others, like Anna Ostroumova-Lebedeva's *Petersburg. The Neva through the Columns of the Stock Exchange* (1908), celebrate the imperial city's monumental neoclassical architecture.

Petersburg's neoclassical architecture emerges as the constant feature of these tributes to the aestheticized capital. The artistic city Benois champions in his paintings and publications is an integrated architectural ensemble of eighteenth-century buildings. The aesthetic fascination with Petersburg's unified architectural front, the city's most obvious and compelling link with its eighteenth-century origins, resulted in a reappraisal of the city, but also of its neoclassical architecture. The most visible shift from a somewhat generic adaptation of European modernism to a unique, indigenous style took place in Russian architecture from 1900 to 1915, when the *style moderne* was slowly supplanted by a neoclassical revival and Russian architects began to view the neoclassical style as a solution to the dilemmas modernism presented.

In *The Origins of Modernism in Russian Architecture*, William Brumfield calls the neoclassical revival in Russian architecture "an extension of modernism, and expression of nostalgia for bygone cultural values, and a reformulated sense of imperial monumentality on a modern urban scale" — a revival characterized by its "stylization" and its "modernized adaptation" (1991, 242). Much of the design in the new revivalist style recalled the architecture of Russia's empire style (*c.* 1820–1830), a period that roughly coincides with the ballet's perceived Golden Age, the romantic era fondly recalled in Fokine's *Chopiniana/Les Sylphides*.

Brumfield documents an influential series of essays and articles that both propagate the new style and testify to its rapid acceptance. Benois began to venerate the neoclassical architecture of "picturesque" Petersburg in 1902 in a series of *Mir iskusstva* essays. The architect Ivan Fomin (1872–1936) followed Benois' tributes with an homage to Moscow's neoclassical architecture in 1904. Four years later, Fomin rejected earlier (*style moderne*) appeals to stylistic plurality and individualism in Russian architecture, favoring instead the united stylistic front of a neoclassical style. (His article on Petersburg neoclassicism appeared in the third volume of Igor Grabar's influential *History of Russian Art* (1912).)

Apollon, which had included reports on new architecture in Petersburg from its first issues, documented the growing interest in the neoclassical revival. Georgy Lukomsky, the journal's architecture critic, was "reassured" by the new classical tendency in architecture in an essay he wrote in a 1910 issue. One year later, at the Fourth Congress of Russian Architects, Lukomsky termed the neoclassical revival "proper." In an essay that appeared in 1913 (the tercentenary of the Romanov dynasty) he argued that the bourgeois period had produced nothing, and that it was necessary to return to previous (classical) canons.

Lukomsky's article was one of several ideological discussions of neoclassical architecture to be found in *Apollon*. N. N. Vrangel's "The Historical Exhibition of Architecture in the Academy of the Arts" and Lukomsky's "Our Architecture from Peter I to Nikolai I" appeared in that journal in 1911, along with Lukomsky's review of Vladimir Shchuko's celebrated neoclassical pavilions for 1911 exhibitions in Rome and Turin. Lukomsky's article "Neo-Classicism in Petersburg Architecture" identified a recent trend (*c.* 1910–1914) of building in Petersburg that the author considered faithful to the origins of the city's architecture: "In architecture now there is a search for primary sources . . . that finds us on the threshold of the study of the very sources that guided the masters of the flowering of Russian classicism" (1914, 9).

Meanwhile, Benois continued to advocate for Russia's neoclassical architecture. With Fomin and Shchuko, he joined the directorate of the Museum of Old Petersburg in 1909 (Borisova *et al.* 1980, 317). By that time, societies were organizing to record and preserve Russian architectural monuments (the architecture of Petersburg, first and foremost). In 1911, the Society of Architect-Artists sponsored an exhibit of Petersburg architecture from Peter I to Nikolai I.

Although art and architecture provide the most striking example of a specifically Russian classical revival in Russian modernism, Russian drama and literature also participated in this renaissance. In the dramatic theater,

Meyerhold's 1917 production of Lermontov's *Masquerade* represented a corresponding interest in Russian "classicism." Even though the Lermontov play is part of the Russian romantic tradition, the play (with Griboedov's *Woe from Wit* and Gogol's *The Inspector General*) represents the beginning of a viable Russian dramatic tradition. Similarly, Meyerhold's lavish staging, reminiscent of the director's 1912 production of Molière's *Don Juan*, effectively conflated the Lermontov play with the European "classics" Meyerhold had already revived.

The poet and playwright Mikhail Kuzmin wrote a number of grand siècle stylizations set in Western Europe, but Michael Green characterizes Kuzmin's *Three Plays* (1907) (*Dangerous Precautions*, *Two Shepherds and a Nymph in a Hut*, and *The Choice of a Bride*) as "a conscious attempt to return to the traditions of the Russian eighteenth century theater" (1973: 254). Kuzmin's nephew and protégé, Sergei Auslender, chose old Petersburg as the backdrop for several of his works. Auslender followed a first collection of stories set in Renaissance Italian and eighteenth-century French locales with a book of stories (published by the Apollon press in 1912) set in early nineteenth-century Petersburg. One of these, "The Night Prince," appeared in the first issue of *Apollon* with illustrations by Dobuzhinsky. The stage adaptation of that story was one of two Auslender plays set in Empire Petersburg and produced in Moscow's Nezlobin Theater (Borisova *et al.*, 1980, 315).

Classical revival in the last years of the Ballets Russes

In the post-war, post-Fokine years the Diaghilev ballet presented a veritable festival of retrospectivist works: *Les Femmes de bonne humeur* (1917), *Pulcinella* and *Le Astuzie femminili* (1920), *The Sleeping Princess* (1921), *Aurora's Wedding* (1922), *Les Tentations de la Bergère* and *Les Fâcheux* (1924), *Zéphire et Flore* (1925), *Ode* and *Apollo* (1928). All were inspired by the past, whether that inspiration manifested itself in music, décor, or dancing.

Western writers on the Diaghilev ballet view this series of works as a manifestation of Western European twentieth-century neo-classicism. Garafola maintains that this style "first emerged in the 1920s" (1989, viii):

> Just as Picasso discovered Ingres after the adventure of cubism, so Diaghilev, in the wake of his futurist experiments, rediscovered the glories of the French classical past. In doing so, he allied the Ballets Russes with a deeply

conservative phenomenon – the retreat by many postwar artists and intellectuals, especially in France, from the firing lines of avant-garde experiment.

(ibid., 116)

Garafola offers the series of concerts of historical French opera given at the Paris Opera in 1915 as the "ideological foundation of retrospective classicism" (ibid.).[7]

Although at first glance the list of Diaghilev's retrospectivist productions might be construed as an homage to eighteenth-century Western European culture, closer inspection reveals clear allusions to the history of Russian ballet and opera. *Le Astuzie femminili* and the divertissement *Cimarosiana* excerpted from it were danced to the music of Domenico Cimarosa, who had served as court composer and conductor for Catherine II. *Zéphire et Flore* was inspired by Charles-Louis Didelot's *Flore et Zéphyre*, first performed in London in 1796 and staged at the Hermitage Theater in St Petersburg in 1808.[8] The eighteenth-century poet Mikhailo Lomonosov's "Evening Meditation on the Greatness of God" [*Vechernee razmyshlenie o bozhiem velichestve*] (1743) inspired the ballet *Ode*. When these allusions to Russian art are considered, a fuller picture of Diaghilev's retrospectivist program emerges. Clearly, much of the movement had Russian, not Western European roots, and Diaghilev's attentions, like those of many Petersburg artists, were shifting to Russian historical subjects.

This phase of Ballets Russes retrospectivism coincides with the stirrings of Diaghilev's final passion: collecting early Russian books. The catalog of the sale of the Diaghilev–Lifar collection (Sotheby Parke Bernet, Monte Carlo, 1975) details the astonishing array of rare volumes that Diaghilev gathered in the last years of his life. Peter I, Catherine II, Cimarosa, and Lomonosov are well represented, as are the majority of important Russian writers of the eighteenth and early nineteenth centuries. The accumulation of Russian "classics," whether first editions of Griboedov, Glinka's manuscripts, or rare copies of Russia's earliest books, recalls Diaghilev's earlier assembling of historical paintings and bespeaks a scholarly undertaking quite similar to that of the "apollonians" whose interest in "classic" literature moved beyond Mir iskusstva eclecticism in this second phase of Russian modernism.

The supreme achievement of this retrospectivist phase, and most obvious reference to the Russian origins of Diaghilev's retrospectivism, was the 1921 production of *Sleeping Beauty*, renamed *The Sleeping Princess* for London and later given in a shortened version as *Aurora's Wedding*. With the

Diaghilev production of *Sleeping Beauty*, Russian retrospectivism had come full circle: the grandly produced Petipa ballet used the traditions of the eighteenth-century court ballet as a point of departure. *Le Pavillon d'Armide*, a précis of *Sleeping Beauty*, had shown the way to the development of the Diaghilev formula. With the 1921 production of *Sleeping Beauty*, Diaghilev presented something close to the original article, the *Gesamtkunstwerk* that first attracted members of the Mir iskusstva group to the ballet.

But in coming full circle Diaghilev reached a dead end. Like Petipa's 1900 ballets and Fokine's *Armide* – all inspired by *Sleeping Beauty* – Diaghilev's production proved less viable than its source and was quickly reduced to a one-act divertissement. The retrospectivist ballets of Petipa and Vsevolozhsky could be accused of following a formula whose credo was period authenticity and whose result was too often *ennui*. The retrospectivist works of the Diaghilev ballet exhibited the usual fault of Ballets Russes productions: a reliance on décor rather than dancing. Garafola calls these works "cocktails mixed in Diaghilev's mind, with design, rather than dance providing the outstanding flavor" (ibid., 120). The ballets of the early, pre-First World War period proved more durable than those of the post-war years, and the ballets in Diaghilev's retrospectivist line bear out this generalization. Of the latter series, only Balanchine's *Apollo* has survived.[9]

Inventing Apollo

Born to a family enmeshed in the fabric of St Petersburg's art worlds,[10] George Balanchine (1904–1983) entered the ballet section of the imperial theater school in St Petersburg in 1913 and graduated from the state theater school in 1921. He joined the state theaters as a dancer that same year and began to choreograph almost immediately. The "Young Ballet" Balanchine helped to organize performed in Petersburg and Moscow from 1922 to 1924 while Balanchine worked as a pianist and dancer in cabarets and cinemas. Balanchine left the Soviet Union in 1924 at the head of a small troupe of young dancers on a Rhineland tour. Electing not to return, the company went to London, where they performed in music halls until Diaghilev hired them later that year.

Balanchine's early career illustrates the degree to which the normally orderly progression from the imperial theater school to the imperial ballet had been disrupted – by revolution, civil war, and the resulting economic chaos in Russia, as well as the enticement of potentially lucrative tours and guest performances in the West. The Ballets Russes was at the height of its powers by the time Balanchine entered the theater school in 1913, and the air of importance that surrounded the touring company represented a powerful lure to young Soviet dancers performing in unheated halls for non-paying audiences of soldiers and factory workers. But the reality of the Diaghilev ballet was considerably less glamorous than the reports that had filtered back to Russia. Balanchine, who had left the Soviet Union because of difficult living conditions there, found himself nearly as impoverished in Western Europe as a member of the celebrated Ballets Russes.

The company's riches remained its collaborators, and Balanchine, like Fokine, was fortunate in this regard. *Apollo* provided Balanchine his first collaboration with Igor Stravinsky – one he later identified as the decisive experience of his early creative life: "*Apollon* I look back on as the turning point of my life. In its discipline and restraint, in its sustained oneness of tone and feelings, the score was a revelation. It seemed to me that I could dare not to use everything, that I, too, could eliminate" (1982, 17).

Stravinsky composed *Apollo* for a festival of contemporary music given in the Library of Congress in 1928. The composer recalled the commission – a ballet of no more than thirty minutes – in his autobiography: "This proposal suited me admirably, for, as I was more or less free just then it enabled me to carry out an idea which had long tempted me, to compose a ballet founded on moments or episodes in Greek mythology plastically interpreted by dancing of the so-called classical school" (1962, 134).

An admirer of ballet and a regular collaborator in Diaghilev's productions, Stravinsky was well-acquainted with the *danse d'école*. Stravinsky had been involved in Diaghilev's 1921 production of *Sleeping Beauty*, orchestrating and arranging several numbers missing from the orchestral score then available in Western Europe. In his memoirs, the composer cites the experience as central to his appreciation of the art of ballet:

> It was a real joy to me to take part in this creation, not only for love of Tchaikovsky but also because of my profound admiration for classical ballet, which in its very essence, by the beauty of it *ordonnance* and the aristocratic austerity of its forms, so closely corresponds with my conception of art. For here, in classical dancing, I see the triumph of studied conception over vagueness, of the rule over the arbitrary, of order over the haphazard. I am thus brought face to face with the eternal conflict in art between the Apollonian and Dionysian principles. The latter assumes ecstasy to be the final goal – that is to say, the losing of oneself – whereas art demands above all the full consciousness of the artist. There can, therefore, be no doubt as to my

choice between the two. And if I appreciate so highly the value of classical ballet, it is not simply a matter of taste on my part, but because I see exactly in it the perfect expression of the Apollonian principle.

(ibid., 99–100)

The apollonian dance Stravinsky admired was none other than the *ballet blanc*, the "white act" divertissement that had promulgated pure, or abstract dance since it became an established part of the romantic ballet. Stravinsky had this image in mind as he was composing his new work:

When, in my admiration for the beauty of line in classical dancing, I dreamed of a ballet of this kind, I had specially in my thoughts what is known as the "white ballet," in which to my mind the very essence of this art reveals itself in all its purity. I found that the absence of many-colored effects and of all superfluities produced a wonderful freshness. This inspired me to write music of an analogous character.

(ibid., 135)

The episode of Greek mythology Stravinsky chose to depict in his ballet was Apollo *musagète* – "that is Apollo as the master of the Muses" (ibid., 134). Stravinsky narrowed the nine muses of mythology to three:

Calliope, receiving the stylus and tablets from Apollo, personifies poetry and its rhythm; Polyhymnia, finger on lips, represents mime. . . . Finally, Terpsichore, combining in herself both the rhythm of poetry and the eloquence of gestures, reveals dancing to the world, and thus among the Muses takes the place of honor beside the Musagetes.

(ibid.)

Stravinsky's libretto describes a Judgment of Paris scenario in which Terpsichore gains Apollo's favor.[11] The muses enter the stage after Apollo's first solo. He dances a pas d'action with them, assigning each a symbol representing her art (a tablet for Calliope, mask for Polyhymnia, and lyre for Terpsichore). The muses dance their variations for Apollo in turn, and Apollo dances a second variation. When he is finished, Terpsichore returns and they dance a pas de deux. The other muses join them in the ballet's coda. The ballet ends when Apollo hears the call from his father, Zeus.[12]

Apollo in the history of ballet

Stravinsky's libretto adapts and abbreviates a favorite plot line of the nineteenth-century ballet: the selection of a mate from a number of suitors, the basic plot of both *Sleeping Beauty* and *Swan Lake*. The ballet also shows similarities to Petipa's 1871 production of *Two Stars* [*Dve zvezdy*] staged for the first benefit performance of Ekaterina Vazem (1848–1937). In her memoirs Vazem recalls the ballet: "These stars were interpreted by [Aleksandra Vergina and myself], and Gerdt played Apollo, who assumed the function of Paris: he was to award a large apple to the better of us. It goes without saying that the stars competed against each other in dances" (1937, 156).[13] Five years later, Petipa choreographed a "mythological ballet," *The Adventures of Peleus* [*Priklyucheniya Peleya*]. That ballet's plot resembled that of Fossano's 1742 ballet *The Golden Apple at the Feast of the Gods and the Judgment of Paris* [*Zolotoe yabloko na pire bogov i sud Parisov*], staged for the court of Empress Elizabeth (Yakovlev 1924, 40). In Fossano's ballet, three goddesses represented the Empresses Catherine I, Anna Ivanovna, and Elizabeth (Lifar n.d., 28).[14]

The Adventures of Peleus was never revived, and *Two Stars* was staged for the last time in 1878, four years before Stravinsky was born. But if the composer never saw these works, his libretto suggests a familiarity with this popular eighteenth- and early nineteenth-century ballet plot: Apollo's test in both the Petipa and the Stravinsky–Balanchine works is a choreographic one.

In the course of the ballet Apollo undergoes a transformation; he is, in Balanchine's words a "wild, half-human youth who acquires nobility through art" (Balanchine and Mason 1977, 26). But Apollo's muses also "derived inspiration from Apollo's teaching" (ibid., 22), according to the choreographer. The model for this ambiguous relationship is probably Fokine's *Les Sylphides*, the most famous of the twentieth century's *ballets blancs*, which also featured one male and three female principal dancers in a "plotless" exercise – a narrative which neither suggests nor precludes concrete relationships among the principal dancers.[15]

Apollo and Louis XIV

The title of the Stravinsky–Balanchine ballet abounds in meanings and implications. Like the journal *Apollon*, the ballet's title asserts the primacy of the apollonian principle in art, a point made clear in the Stravinsky quote cited earlier. The ballet's title also signals the return of the male dancer as ballet protagonist. Male dancers had been reduced to supporting roles in the ballets of the nineteenth century, nearly disappearing from Western European stages as female dancers *en travesti* took over their roles and eponymous heroines were the rule.[16] In the Ballets Russes, ballets featuring male protagonists (usually Nijinsky) tended toward depictions of sexually ambiguous males (*Narcisse*, *Le Spectre de la rose*) or sub-human ones (*Faune*, *Petrushka*).[17]

The return of the male dancer in a heroic mode recalled the ballet of the grand siècle, when the popularity of male dancers such as Louis Dupré and Auguste Vestris equaled or surpassed that of their female counterparts. The most famous dancer of the day, Louis XIV, had himself taken the part of Apollo in *Le Ballet de la nuit* (1653), a fact duly noted by *Apollo*'s collaborators. Stravinsky admitted that the ballet had as much to do with French neoclassicism as with Greek antiquity: "*Apollo* is a tribute to the French seventeenth century," . . ."the chariot, the three horses, and the sun disc were the emblem of the roi du soleil" (1962, 10). Balanchine concurred: "It wasn't meant to be Greek, it was meant to be French. Apollo is Louis XIV, le roi soleil, leader of the muses and himself a dancer" (Harris 1982, 20).[18]

In conflating these classical Greek and neoclassical French traditions, Stravinsky and Balanchine unite the two main strands of Russian twentieth-century retrospectivism. Twenty years earlier, such a conflation would have been impossible: Benois' watercolor renderings of Versailles and Duncan's Greek dances had little in common. But Stravinsky's and Balanchine's conception of classicism had less to do with stylization and imitation than with organization and construction. Stravinsky discussed his view of classicism in a 1927 essay:

> There is much talk of a return to classicism nowadays, and works believed to have been influenced by works deemed "classical" are termed "neoclassical." It is difficult to say whether this classification is in fact justified. Might this not be the result of an investigation more profound (at least in works worthy of attention – works that reveal the visible influence of earlier works) than the simple imitation of a so-called classical language?
>
> This does not constitute neo-classicism, since classicism could never be characterized by technical methods (which change now as they do in every period) but rather by the merits of its construction.
>
> (1927: 13–14)

Like their predecessors in the journal *Apollon*, anxious to restore balance to Russia's dionysian hellenism, Stravinsky and Balanchine turned to classical ideals. The backward glance in *Apollo* is the "momentary enthusiasm" Makovsky described; the retrospectivist conceit is far less important than the future the ballet foreshadows. *Apollo* can be called a "classical" ballet because its Ancient Greek and neoclassical French sources are no longer incongruous: the ballet's theme refers to a classical ideal, rather than a time or place. With this reconciliation to the art of the past, Stravinsky and Balanchine declared a new classicism for the ballet, sanctioned by the ballet's own history and tradition, no longer needful of ancient chronological antecedents.

Balanchine's Apollo

Apollo and the Faun

Writing in 1947, Lincoln Kirstein asserted that "[Serge Lifar's] performance in [*Apollo*] was unrivaled since Nijinsky's Faun of sixteen years before" (40). Kirstein's reference to Nijinsky's ballet makes for an unusual comparison. Stylistically, the works are polar opposites. But *Faune* represented the most extreme example of the new ballet's anti-academicism to all but the few who remembered *Sacre* (which vanished from the repertory after nine performances). Balanchine's *Apollo*, the ballet that reconciled the two strands of twentieth-century retrospectivism would take up the thread of Russia's ballet tradition, beginning where the last important work in that line left off.

Only five days before the première of Balanchine's ballet, Lifar danced the lead in Nijinsky's. Lubov Tchernicheva, Balanchine's Calliope, was Lifar's lead nymph. Appropriately enough, Balanchine's *Apollo* begins by restating the moment of Nijinsky's ballet that Minsky characterized as a capitulation to Dionysus: "Apollo cedes place to Dionysus – and the curtain rings down." As Balanchine's *Apollo* is currently performed, that scenario is reversed: the curtain rises on the "half-human" youth whose dionysian excesses cede place to Apollonian restraint.[19]

Despite their stylistic incongruities, Nijinsky's *Faune* and Balanchine's *Apollo* show structural similarities. Both feature a male protagonist who chooses one woman from a small group. Both ballets are quasi-narrative, with easily understood, minimal plots. But Balanchine's very dissimilar realization of the basic plot represents a visceral, conscious response to the Nijinsky work. His revisions of *Apollo* over the next fifty years suggest a life-long dialog with Nijinsky's ballet and the aesthetic it came to represent.

As *Faune* held its place in the repertory, Balanchine continued to revive and revise *Apollo*.

Read as a manifesto of a new kind of modernist ballet (and a comment on Nijinsky's), Balanchine's *Apollo* charts two separate progressions. First, the ballet supplants the dionysian sensuality of Nijinsky's work with a classical apollonian purity. Second, the work's explicit contrasts of two- and three-dimensional movement in space emend Nijinsky's experiment.

Rebuilding the academy

Apollo's variation, now the first in the ballet, is cast in a decidedly dionysian mode. The movement lacks the finesse and polish of an ordinary classical variation: its phrases start and stop abruptly. Apollo travels from right to left and from front to back of the stage, his primarily linear trajectories offering a primitive approximation of the embellished diagonal and circular paths of the male dancer's more typical classical variation. The variation shows the young god in a process of self-discovery. Apollo scrutinizes his strength, leap, flexion, and mobility; the anatomized movements recall those of the Faun – in Garafola's words, "movements that revealed the phylogeny of ballet" (1989, 57). As the ballet unfolds, Apollo's gradual mastery of "three-dimensional" movement and his increasing use of the entire stage space convey his process of maturation choreographically.

Apollo ends his variation at the center of the stage. The muses emerge from the wings, approaching him from three corners of the stage. As they enter, Apollo turns in attitude, a pose that accentuates the body's three-dimensionality. As Apollo turns, the muses are drawn to him, as though pulled. The three-dimensional figure Apollo describes contrasts the flattened poses and movement along single planes in his variation – poses and movement patterns that allude to the constraint of Nijinsky's work. Apollo's moving pose both acknowledges the stage's dimensions and reifies the three-dimensional potential of his own body.

This juxtaposition of two- and three-dimensionality speaks to the ballet's central theme. The increasing eloquence of Apollo's movement signals a return to the basic principles of the *danse d'école*, the return to a more traditional "academic" use of the body in the performance space, a reassessment of the dancing body's place within the spatial dimensions of the stage. Since the ballet academy had developed over centuries to best present the dancing body on the stage, Balanchine's simultaneous exploration of the classical vocabulary and the stage space are intrinsically related – in the same way that Nijinsky's *Faune* and *Sacre* declared the invalidity of both these ballet fundamentals.

The pas d'action, the danced quasi-narrative sections that follow, examines the three-dimensional, architectural potential of the human form. When the muses reach Apollo they stand around him, right hands raised in salute behind his head (Illustration 2). This figure is repeated, with variations, twice in the section. In the next of these, the muses face the kneeling Apollo, extending their legs in high arabesque as Apollo raises the lute. The final variation on this pose comes at the end of the pas d'action. This time, the muses (again in arabesque) face outward. This sequence establishes an important motif of the choreography: the expansion of movement, from self-contained to expansive poses, from spatially intro-spective movement to choreography that covers the stage.

Repeatedly, the muses form straight lines that Apollo breaks, urging them into non-linear, three-dimensional formations. These sequences allude to moments in *Faune*: when the faun tries to join the nymph's games, he only scatters them, disrupting the linear groupings they form across the stage. The muses divulge their movement secrets to Apollo in these sequences, and in the variations that follow. As Apollo prods the muses out of their self-contained planes, they reveal the body in its fully realized, three-dimensional form.

The muses' variations follow the pas d'action. Those for Calliope and Polyhymnia, though difficult, are hardly eloquent. Repeated percussive thumps in the score punctuate Calliope's variation, "caesurae" Balanchine translates into bodily contractions (Croce 1982, 114). Polyhymnia dances her variation with a finger to her lips, a metaphor of mime's silence that constrains movement as well.

Terpsichore's variation differs from those of her sister muses in its fluidity and deceptive ease. Holding the lyre above her head as she enters, and echoing its curves with her arms, Terpsichore twists her body sinuously as her feet lightly paw the ground before her. As she puts the lyre down and executes a series of rapid turns, the expressive use of her free arms distin-guishes her movement from that of the other muses. The unrestricted use of the upper body is the secret of Terpsichore's allure, and a choreographic state-ment on the development of dance classicism: *épaulement*, the opposition of the shoulders, head, and arms to the central axis of the body (the ballet's answer to *contrapposto*), distinguished nineteenth-century Russian dancing from that of any other European school. Terpsichore's turns, with

their sophisticated positioning of the head and shoulders, pay tribute to Petipa's academy, and his contribution to the art. Like those compiling the first histories of the Russian arts, Balanchine acknowledges the distinctly Russian contributions to the Western art form in Terpsichore's choreography.

Apollo's second variation follows Terpsichore's. The quality of the movement, though brusque, reveals a more sophisticated spatial orientation than that of the first variation: there are more turns, the body is displayed from all sides. After completing the variation, Apollo sits momentarily, right arm extended back as in the ballet's first pose. But here, autoeroticism has no place: Terpsichore enters, touching his finger in a gesture connoting inspiration surely borrowed from Michaelangelo. Terpsichore completes the pose, the line described by his arm lengthens and extends to the heavens through her upward gesture.

The pas de deux that follows is a lesson in complementary movement, a study of the body's geometric and mechanical possibilities (and a prelude to the extreme examination of interdependent strength and balance in the pas de deux of Balanchine's *Agon* (1957)). Calliope and Polyhymnia return at the end of the pas de deux. Their movements echo many of Terpsichore's gestures, yet their unison repetition suggests a kind of deficiency, a lame recitation of Terpsichore's eloquent speech.

The ballet's final movement passage illustrates the ballet's conquest of space most clearly. As the muses sit side by side, legs extended to the front and touching, Apollo stands behind them and extends his hand over their heads. As each muse raises one leg Apollo holds them together briefly. He then forms a circle with his arm and each links their arms around his. Their arms interlocked, the muses stand, one by one. The cluster they form, once small, continues to grow as they circle around one another, eventually breaking apart. These circles recall a moment in the pas d'action when Terpsichore circles as if in orbit around Apollo and the muses. Repeated and enlarged in the coda, the movement sequence underscores the ballet's motif of three-dimensional conquest. At the end of this sequence, the four walk across the stage in distinct planes, again recalling Nijinsky's choreography.

The four join again in the ballet's final pose – a sunburst formed as the muses lean against Apollo and each extends a leg in arabesque as Apollo gestures toward the heavens (Illustration 3). Like Apollo's first position, the pose is flat, a silhouette, but its dramatic opening suggests a spatial complexity that Nijinsky's ballet had abjured as the "rays" of the sun round out and complete the promise of the ballet's opening scene (see Illustration 1).[20]

Apollo returns to his original, flattened pose twice during the ballet;

once when Terpsichore's touch extends the line indicated by Apollo's arm, and then at the end, when the flatness of the original pose is given added dimension as the "rays" of legs open. These subtle references to Nijinsky's ballet, with its voided perspectives and static movement, are more than allusions to *Faune*. As the flat poses become fully dimensional, they reveal the body's potential for movement in space.

In charting Apollo's trajectory, from the half-human boy engaged in a dionysian act as the curtain opens, to young god at the ballet's end, Balanchine makes several pithy comments on the state of the ballet academy. The work speaks to the importance of the academy, the value of its movement vocabulary and its potential to incorporate new types of movement (as Balanchine does in the ballet). The ballet also makes an eloquent case for a reconsideration of the stage space. No longer dependent on the previous century's illusionistic stage sets, Balanchine focuses on the architectural properties of the dancing bodies, and their ability to manipulate volumes of space around them.

Rouben Ter Arutunian, the scenic designer who frequently collaborated with Balanchine, wrote: "The stage space, when left without movement, is essentially perceived by the audience in two dimensions. It is the movement of the dancers that reveals to them the presence of the third dimension" (quoted in Armstrong and Morgan 1984, 9). Bakst had revived the use of false perspective in his designs for the 1921 staging of *Sleeping Beauty* (Levinson 1921, 134); Balanchine's choreography for *Apollo* signaled a new approach to the use of the stage space. Balanchine's stage is not fixed, but constantly redefined by the movement of the bodies dancing on it. The ballet's groupings – the constant shifts from single to multiple planes – stress the work's central priority: the exploration of the space for dance. The ballet's final movement sequence, culminating in the sunburst pose, provides the most compelling example.

Through *Apollo* Lincoln Kirstein came to understand dance as "an independent language of visual plastic interest based on music unadorned. The preoccupation was with three-dimensional movement measured by opulent rhythm and sonority" (1979, 62). The ballet's preoccupation with stage space and the return to a relatively classical movement vocabulary amount to a reinvention of the academy, a return to the ballet's basic priorities. Arlene Croce has observed that "by 1928 . . . Balanchine could use academic technique in *Apollo* as Nijinsky had used anti-academicisms in *Faune* – for the purpose of asserting cardinal priorities of substance over decoration, invention over representation" (1982, 108).[21]

In *Apollon* in 1909, Bakst predicted that "the ideals of future painting will coincide with the ideals of the schools of antiquity" (II, 61):

> The art of the future will turn to the cult of man, his nudity.
>
> Artists will seek new inspiration in the forms of the nude body, and we will return, like the Greeks of the Periclean period, to their view of the beauty of nature.
>
> They placed the beautiful, nude human body first. For the Greeks, gods, goddesses, heroes and mere mortals were only a pretext for the celebration of the naked body. . . . The art of the future will return to this!
>
> (II, 60–61)

Apollo's minimal austerity and clarity of execution answer Bakst's call for a return to man and a naked, lapidary style. But the "nudity" of the Balanchine–Stravinsky work was formal, not literal. Where Bakst urged a return to the human figure, Balanchine and Stravinsky returned to an equally essential foundation: the vocabulary and syntax of the classical academy. Almost twenty years after Bakst's prediction, *Apollo* realized the aesthetic prognoses of *Apollon*.

6

BODIES
AND
BUILDINGS

N EAR THE end of his long, two-part article, "The Paths of Classicism in Art," Lev Bakst proclaims: "The air, the sun, and foliage are the elements of recent painting; the elements of the future will be man and stone" (1909, II, 61). Throughout the essay that appeared in the second and third issues of *Apollon*, Bakst stresses the importance of the nude human form for the art of the future and is heartened by the work of his contemporaries. "Around us . . . we see indications of laudatory investigation in this direction, in the isolation and emphasis on man's beauty, unencumbered by the details and the landscape that had crushed it" (ibid., 60).

For evidence of this rediscovery of the body, Bakst turns to the dance, familiar territory for one who had participated in its twentieth-century renaissance. Yet Bakst describes the dance event as a naïve spectator:

> A concert hall, a full house, enjoying the rhythmic – seemingly monotonous – skipping of a danseuse for an entire evening.
> The whole aim of this entirely new type of choreography consists of creating as diverse a number of plastic poses as possible and to draw attention to the beauty of the lines of an artistically-created human nudity.
>
> (ibid.)

The art of the future would indeed return to "the cult of man" as Bakst predicted. But the "nudity" Bakst foresaw would never be realized in any literal sense, as twentieth-century visual artists largely abandoned the figure. Rather, Bakst's "nudity" would be realized in the abstraction and formalism of twentieth-century art – most literally in the dance Bakst pretended not to understand. The "pure" (non-narrative) movement Bakst describes, the focus on plastic "poses" rather than on plot or décor, and the inherent beauty of the "nude" human body became salient features of the ballets Balanchine began to create some twenty years after the publication of Bakst's essay.

The architecture of acmeism

The journal *Apollon* emerged as the primary voice of Russia's modernist movement in 1909, when its major competitors, the symbolist journals *Vesy* [Libra] and *Zolotoe runo* [The Golden Fleece], ceased publication. The internecine debates that marked the passing of Russian symbolism as a viable poetic movement were carried out on *Apollon*'s pages in 1910, the same year that two seminal essays heralding poetry's next wave appeared on its pages: Mikhail Kuzmin's "On Beautiful Clarity" [*O prekrasnoy yasnosti*] and Nikolai Gumilyov's "The Life of Verse" [*Zhizn' stikha*]. Beginning as an ecumenical journal of Russia's modernist movement, *Apollon* rapidly became the chief venue of a new group of poets calling themselves "acmeists."

The poets associated with the acmeist movement – Nikolai Gumilyov, Sergei Gorodetsky, Anna Akhmatova, Osip Mandelshtam, Vladimir Narbut, Mikhail Zenkevich – first associated as members of the Poet's Guild [Cekh poetov], a circle that formed in 1911. The new group derived its name from the Greek *akme* – the highest degree. Their poetry stressed clarity of exposition, eschewing the vagueness, obscurity and mysticism of symbolist poetry in favor of finely crafted verse based on tangible human experience.

The models the poets adopted to metaphorize their poetics characterize the aesthetic shift from symbolism to acmeism. Russian symbolists, like their French predecessors, admired the sonorance and subjectivity of music and strove to imitate its effects. (Andrei Bely wrote prose "symphonies.") For the symbolists, music was inherently non-utilitarian, "aesthetic," and uniquely capable of synthesizing other media. (Of course, both music and poetry exist in time, and both, in performance, are aural.)

The favorite metaphor of acmeist theorists was an architectural one, a model whose appropriateness for poetic identification is considerably more problematic, as architecture exists in time and space, precluding direct imitation. But the acmeists did not advocate symbolist synaesthesia. Architecture provided a source of emulation (rather than imitation) for the acmeists.

Reviewing *Stone*, Osip Mandelshtam's first collection of poems, Gumilyov noted:

> This love for everything living and solid leads O. Mandelshtam to archi-
> tecture. He loves buildings as much as other poets love mountains or the sea.
> And he describes them in detail, finds parallels between them and himself, and
> builds universal theories on the basis of their lines.

> (1914, 127)

In "Notre Dame," a poem from that collection, Mandelshtam characterizes gothic architecture as an ideal combination of art and engineering, beauty and utility in its synthesis of form and content. The cathedral also represents a tangible link to past art and civilization. The past-tense verbs in the first lines of Mandelshtam's most famous "architectural" poems, "Notre Dame" and "Hagia Sophia," stress these monuments' historical significance: "Where Roman courts judged a foreign people," "Hagia Sophia, here god judged men and tsars!" (1928, 40, 42).[1]

The architectural metaphor became a salient feature of acmeist theory from the first phases of its formulation. Kuzmin's "On Beautiful Clarity" praised apollonian art and lamented the lack of a prose academy, using architectural paradigms to sound a call for clarity over obscurity in literature:

> We study, as it were, the laying of stones in the building whose architect we
> wish to become. And we must have a vigilant eye, a true hand, and a clear
> sense of regularity, perspective, and proportion to achieve the desired result.
> It is necessary, that the entire construction does not collapse from a
> poorly-placed vault, and that the parts do not overshadow the whole, so that
> the most asymmetrical, worrisome scheme is achieved by conscious and
> orderly means. Then it will be a work of art about which it may be said: "ars
> long, vita brevis." It is essential, apart from ingenious talent, to have a
> knowledge of one's material and form, and the correspondences between it
> and content.

> (1910, 7)

Kuzmin articulated several of the key tenets of the new movement in his essay, using architectural metaphors to underscore the importance of literary craftsmanship. The emphasis on perspective and proportion elevates the discussion of craftsmanship to the realm of artistic creation, focusing on the blend of art and utility that made the architectural example so appealing to the acmeists. Mandelshtam's "The Morning of Acmeism" [*Utro akmeizma*], written in 1913, elaborates and extends Kuzmin's architectural metaphor:

> Acmeism is for those, who, seized with the spirit of building, don't shirk from its heaviness, and gladly accept it in order to awaken and utilize its dormant architectural strength. The architect says: "I build, therefore I am right."
>
> (1987, 169)

Mandelshtam echoes Kuzmin in implying a distinction between craft and art, building and creation. The acmeist artist must first be a craftsman, knowledgeable of his materials, and possess the courage to effect their transformation.

Kuzmin's discussion of literary material anticipates Gumilyov's discussion of the word in poetry and Mandelshtam's formulation of "logos," both of which stress the denotative power of the word. Mandelshtam insists that the "reality" of the material (the word, for a poet) is key to his elevation of the logos, the "conscious sense of the word" to the level of importance that music held for the symbolists. The author emphasizes the transformation of material as its potential is realized and its rightful place in an artistic structure is found.

> What lunatic would agree to build if he did not believe in the reality of the material whose resistance he must overcome. The stone in the hands of the architect is transformed into substance.
>
> [The stone] itself uncovered its hidden potential for dynamism, as if it begged to join the crossed vault, to participate in the joyful interaction of its peers.
>
> (1987, 169)

Finally, Mandelshtam speaks of the necessary conditions for proper building/creation. His emphases on artistic creation within the natural limitations of the form are a touchstone of acmeist theory. The tone of the essay is heroic, recalling the movement's early "Adamist" phase, when poets (especially Sergei Gorodetsky) advocated a fresh ("first man's") world view:

> In order to build successfully, the first condition is a sincere piety for the three dimensions of space – to look upon them neither as a burden nor an unfortunate occurrence, but as a God-given palace. . . . It is possible to build

only in the name of the "three dimensions," since they are the condition of all architecture. . . . To build is to wage war against emptiness, to hypnotize space. The great arrow of the Gothic bell tower is evil because its entire existence is to stab the sky, to reproach it for its emptiness.

(ibid., 170)

Although the acmeist movement was short-lived, owing to war, revolution, and the cultural chaos that followed, surviving members continued to identify themselves as acmeists (Akhmatova as late as 1961), and the group's theoretical writings continued to be published. Mandelshtam's seminal essay "On the Nature of the Word" [*O prirode slova*] was not published until 1922; "The Morning of Acmeism" [*Utro akmeizma*] was published in 1919 and reprinted in 1929. Gumilyov's critical essays on Russian poetry (from *Apollon*) were published together in 1923. The collection reiterated the main features of early acmeist theory, extending the movement's influence well into the 1920s.

The poetic movement that took shape on the pages of *Apollon* constructed a theoretical framework that would also elucidate the poetics of George Balanchine's choreography. Mandelshtam's guild of artisans, a recurring metaphor of acmeist theory, is the literary analog of the ballet academy, to which Balanchine would also return. These academies, storehouses of time-honored trade secrets, provided both the poets and the choreographer the essential preconditions of artistic creation: a workmanlike understanding of materials and conditions.

Balanchine and the acmeists

Most scholars agree that Balanchine's choreography brings ballet fully into the realm of the modern, though there is considerable debate as to how this is accomplished. In forging closer links to the dance's musical accompaniment and rejecting décor as an intrinsic feature of his choreography, Balanchine's aesthetic became distinct from that of Petipa (for whom movement could take precedence over music) or Diaghilev (who typically sought an ideal linkage of the arts). In Balanchine's theater, dance could be said to accompany the music (where the opposite could be true of nineteenth-century ballet), and seldom cedes place to décor (as was often the case in the Diaghilev ballet).

In an article first published in 1973, David Michael Levin discusses

Balanchine's formalism as a tension maintained between weight and weightlessness that both acknowledges and transcends gravity (1983, 123–124). Marshall Cohen disagrees with this formulation. He feels that Levin's argument fails to account for the three-dimensionality of the dancing body (ibid., 171). But the state of grace Levin sees in the "tense simultaneity" of weight and weightlessness (ibid., 124) and Cohen's assertion of the dancing body in three-dimensional space are neither incompatible nor mutually exclusive. Indeed, these features of Balanchine's choreography link his work to that of Russia's acmeist poets. In the lucidity of his themes and their execution, in the incorporation of vernacular movement and gestures, and the return to the fundamental principles of the *danse d'école*, Balanchine's choreography represents a balletic response to acmeist poetics.

Western dance historians, anxious to place Balanchine's work in the context of Russian art and culture, have generally looked to the "vanguard" art of the early Soviet period as the source of Balanchine's innovation (particularly since the publication of Christina Lodder's *Russian Constructivism* in 1983). Those who would draw parallels to constructivism in Balanchine's work frequently cite Balanchine's famous quote "I don't create or invent anything, I assemble" (Cott 1983, 133) as does Margaret Thompson Drewal, who uses the quote as the epigraph to her article "Constructionist Concepts in Balanchine's Choreography." Robert Johnson, who, like Garafola, views *Apollo* as part of a Western European return to classicism after the war, uses constructivism to explain the "formal emphasis of the ultraclassical *Apollon*" (1985, 53).[2]

Balanchine did participate in constructivist choreographic experiments in his years with Diaghilev. He choreographed *La Chatte* (1927) around the constructivist stage set designed by Naum Gabo and Anton Pevsner. *Prodigal Son* (1929) is quite obviously influenced by constructivist aesthetics, with its machine-age dances for the "friends," and its use of a single prop as fence, table, ship, and cross. But Balanchine's revivals of *Apollo* pared away the work's constructivist touches (the multi-planar staging of the birth scene and the apotheosis), leaving the choreography to impart the action, as befits a balletic treatment of the Apollo theme. Although constructivism did play a role in the choreographer's Diaghilev-era work, constructivist aesthetics inform little of Balanchine's choreography after his association with the impresario ended. (Balanchine was only twenty-five when Diaghilev died in 1929.)

Soviet studies of Balanchine's early work discuss the possible influence of Moscow's vanguard art, constructivist theater, and the work of Kasian

Goleizovsky, an innovative Moscow choreographer, on the early work of Balanchine (Slonimsky 1975–1976; Suritz 1990a, 73–78). In "The Young Balanchine in Russia," (1990b) Suritz lists a number of Soviet choreographers (primarily from Moscow) whose works Balanchine might have seen in St Petersburg. Suritz speculates that many of these artists "made an impression" on Balanchine, but is unable to draw direct correspondences to any of Balanchine's mature work.[3]

It is important to remember that the period in question was both a relatively brief and very early one for the choreographer, who graduated from the ballet school at seventeen in 1921 and left the Soviet Union three years later, when he was only twenty. A 1924 review of a performance of Balanchine's Young Ballet advises the choreographer to "find himself':

> [Balanchine's] efforts at imitating Lukin and Goleizovsky I considered a fundamental error. . . . I am sure that the young choreographer will be able to extricate himself from this state of rebellious restlessness and will fulfill his talents without the assistance of the Moscow decadents.
>
> (Gvozdev 1990, 76)

Ironically, that review chronicled the last of the Young Ballet's performances. Balanchine's next works were created for the Diaghilev company during a five-year period that served as Balanchine's choreographic apprenticeship (and his acquaintance with Diaghilev's European "world of art"). In a videotaped interview included in the PBS documentary on Balanchine's life and works (see Appendix, p. 135), the choreographer discusses this period as the most important in his education and formation as a choreographer. His self-described turning point, *Apollo*, came in 1928, when he was only twenty-four. (The story of *Apollo* – the young god's attainment of nobility through art – thus becomes an autobiographical account of the young choreographer's encounters with yet unfamiliar muses.)

Lincoln Kirstein asserted that Balanchine's "youthful insecurities lay entirely in questions of taste, never in technique." He continued:

> The taste of Balanchine when he settled in France was the taste of a young Soviet Romantic revolutionary of his period – the epoch of Miaskovsky, the Suprematists and Constructivists, the first Cultural Program of Lunacharsky. He adored Rachmaninoff and Scriabin; yet until Diaghileff showed him the Louvre and Italy he had hardly noticed painting . . . Balanchine's taste was developed, and even to a certain degree formed, by Diaghileff.
>
> (1947, 37, 38)

111

The theory and practice of the acmeist poets offers a more plausible Russian link to the Balanchine aesthetic than that of Moscow's vanguard artists. Like Balanchine, the acmeists were a Petersburg phenomenon whose poetics develop the backward glance that characterized Petersburg art from the turn of the century. Acmeism represented a corrective to the poetry of their symbolist predecessors, not a revolt, and Balanchine's choreography, while opposing the aesthetic of Fokine, grew from it organically in a similar fashion. If any clear distinction can be drawn between the Moscow and St Petersburg art of the early twentieth century, it rests in their basic attitude toward the art of the past. In this respect, the œuvres of Balanchine and the acmeists are clearly linked.

Balanchine was a child when the acmeists were formulating the theoretic basis of their movement in St Petersburg, but his family background provided him a degree of cultural access early on. He was born to a family well-connected to the city's artistic culture (his uncle had studied at the Academy of Arts with Konstantin Makovsky, father of Sergei, the founder and editor of *Apollon*, and his own father was a well-known composer). As a student, Balanchine appeared more frequently on the stage of the Aleksandrinsky (dramatic) Theater than at the Maryinsky, and he familiarized himself with the repertory of the Russian dramatic stage as well as the ballet repertory (Slonimsky 1975–1976, 1, 6). His first acquaintance with acmeist poetry probably came while he was a student in the theater school. Balanchine's contemporary, Yuri Slonimsky, recalls that Akhmatova was widely read in the ballet school *c.* 1919, as were Mayakovsky and Esenin (ibid., 16–18). Slonimsky includes several acmeists in his list of ballet's "regulars":

> At the ballet performances in those years one could see many poets, Alexander Blok, Anna Akhmatova, Osip Mandelshtam, Mikhail Kuzmin; and during visits to Petrograd, Vladimir Mayakovsky and Sergei Esenin. . . . The list of balletomanes of those years – artists, writers, architects, scholars, military men, doctors – is enormous. Their impassioned influence on the young ballet contributed in no small measure to an infusion of intellectual oxygen, to an enrichment of the spiritual climate of the ballet theater.[4]
>
> (ibid., 14)

An album of poetry and drawings dedicated to the ballerina Tamara Karsavina lends credence to Slonimsky's assertion. In March 1914, Petersburg visual artists and poets compiled an album with poems and drawings to present to the dancer at an evening held in her honor at the cabaret "The Stray Dog" [Brodyachaya sobaka]. Akhmatova, Gumilyov,

Lozinsky, and Kuzmin each contributed a poem. (Clearly, the cultural milieu of the Petersburg ballet in Balanchine's time differed from the "somewhat eccentric and slightly depraved" following Russia's late nineteenth-century ballet enjoyed (Benois 1941, 47).)

Balanchine spoke of the acmeists and their work in the years immediately preceding his death. In a series of interviews conducted by the musicologist Solomon Volkov in 1981 and 1982 (published three years later as *Balanchine's Tchaikovsky*), Balanchine recalls being introduced to Akhmatova. "I loved her poetry. I have it" (Volkov 1985, 68). He also remembered his collaboration with Kuzmin on a play staged by Sergei Radlov at the Aleksandrinsky Theater. (Kuzmin wrote the music for the dances Balanchine staged.)

By the time Balanchine arrived in Western Europe, he was well acquainted with both the nineteenth-century ballet academy and its twentieth-century amendments. The choreographic legacy that Balanchine inherited included Petipa classics learned at the ballet school and performed in the state theaters as well as works of experimental choreographers such as Fyodr Lopukhov and Kasian Goleizovsky.

But Balanchine's choreography amounts to a reappraisal of the creative process, a reappraisal that focused on the material employed in the composition and on its form.

In 1927 Balanchine's life-long collaborator, Igor Stravinsky, wrote:

> The thing in itself (a theme or a rhythm in music, for example) is not sufficient material for the creation of a work of art. It is clear that this material must still find that reciprocal arrangement that in music, as in all the arts, is called form. All great works of art are distinguished by this quality – a quality of the correspondence of things, the correspondence of the material.
>
> (1927: 13–14)

Stravinsky's understanding of form in artistic creation echoes the main lines of acmeist theory, especially the writings of Kuzmin, Mandelshtam, and Gumilyov. His emphasis of form and the dialogue between compositional and formal elements also inform Balanchine's choreography, with its similar rethinking of the basic conditions and limitations of dance, its reappraisal of the material (the human body), and the craft of its composition.

In discussing the first phase of Russian retrospectivism (*c.* 1890–1910), it has been sufficient to describe correspondences among the various art forms in terms of thematic similarities. Whether ballets or poems took on

French neoclassical or Ancient Greek stylizations at the turn of the century, their basic structures and vocabularies remained fundamentally unchanged. In discussing the works of Balanchine and acmeists (and the correspondences between them) substance, not style, becomes the central issue. The correspondences between the work of the acmeist poets and Balanchine center around formal, rather than thematic, concerns.

Acmeist architecture in Balanchine's choreography

In "Balanchine: The Early Years," Yuri Slonimsky digresses from his discussion of Balanchine's early training in Russia to describe the place where that training took place, the imperial theater school on St Petersburg's Rossi (Theater) Street:

> Wherever students or performers living and rehearsing on Rossi Street might turn . . . they cannot remain indifferent to Rossi's distinctive and . . . musical sense of rhythm. . . . The entire street consists of a single building on each side. It is as if one were proceeding triumphantly along a broad corridor to the Muses. As one approaches the theater, the columns, after fusing with each other, disassociate themselves. They unexpectedly become alive, acquire an alternating cadence with the windows and become participants in the musical-rhythmic movement. . . . The passersby are caught up in a theatrical presentation. They are infected with the music and rhythm of the architectural ensemble and penetrate into its simplicity and majesty. It begins to seem that in the repetitions of columns on both sides, Rossi has constructed, with the art of a ballet master, the rows of a corps de ballet. And in the spaces between then, in the window recesses, it is as if he has selected the "places" of the soloists contributing their "voices" to the measured, uniform pace of the columns. This ensemble seems related somehow to the composition of the corps de ballet of classical productions.
>
> When a student absorbs this orderly procession from day to day and from year to year, he becomes possessed by its beauty. Without Rossi Street our ballet, it seems to me, would be poorer. The dancing of the finest ballerinas of the city on the Neva is somehow indebted to it and to its inimitable lines. And is not Balanchine, with his passion for neoclassicism, also indebted to it?
>
> (1975–1976, 4–5)

The influence of St Petersburg's neoclassical architecture on that city's early twentieth-century art and artists remains a fascinating and under-studied facet of Russian modernism. A commonplace of early acmeist

114

theory, architectural metaphors also inform much of Balanchine's choreography. The titles of works such as *Le Palais de cristal* and the suggestions of gardens and palaces in others hint at this. More importantly, Balanchine's use of the moving human body in three-dimensional space elucidates the architectural paradigms the acmeists used to explain their aesthetic program. The architectural aspects of Balanchine's choreography represent practical solutions to the basic issues and problems of the ballet master's craft. Like Mandelshtam, Balanchine focuses first on his material and second on that material's potential interactions within the larger structure of his composition.

Logos

The discussion of the material of poetry occupied a central place in the development of acmeist theory. Mandelshtam's essays – "The Morning of Acmeism" (first published in 1919), "The Word and Culture" (1921), and "On the Nature of the Word" (1922) – propose a conception of the word as ultimate reality: "The word as such is this reality of poetry. . . . For the acmeists, the conscious sense of the word, the Logos, is as splendid a form as music is for the symbolists" (1987, 168–169).

In his discussion of Mandelshtam's important early poem "Notre Dame," Peter Steiner calls the poet's understanding of "the word" a compromise: "the literal meaning of the word was to be an integral part of it, but the word as a whole was to function as an organism, a dynamic, semantic entity" (1977, 241). Steiner continues: "The rejection of the boundless Symbolist mystery of the word and the emphasis on its dynamic concreteness thus led Mandelshtam to a new concept of the word – as the *material* for poetry" (ibid., 242)

Balanchine arrived at a similar understanding of the dancing body's materiality in his choreography. Where Petipa and Diaghilev's choreographers regarded costumes, décor, and music as essential features of their ballets, Balanchine settled on a simpler formula. The human body and its movement in time through space came to be primary: time (expressed through music) and space would become the fundamental conditions of dance composition.

The comparatively high regard Balanchine held for the body as a compositional element may be seen in the development of a particularly Balanchinian "uniform" for dancing. The clothes that costume many of the choreographer's late works (and some of the early ones) resemble the simplified dress dancers wear in daily classes and rehearsals, and were adopted for the same reasons: the leotard and tights allow maximal freedom of movement for the dancer and allow the viewer an unobstructed view of the workings of the body.

Costume reform had been an important feature of the new ballet: Isadora Duncan's unshod feet and "free" torso demonstrated the kinetic potential of the unbound body, Fokine's costume reforms aimed at deconventionalizing the ballet costume. But the innovation of Balanchine's costuming resides in its austere simplicity. Neither scandalous nor evocative, Balanchine's "black and white" costumes are designed not to be noticed.

The costumes used in the majority of Balanchine's "modernist" works gave their name to a genre of Balanchine ballets: the sparse, minimalist works of Balanchine's American period are known as "black and white" ballets. These include the greater share of the Stravinsky ballets and modern classics such as *The Four Temperaments* and *Episodes*. *Apollo* and *The Four Temperaments* were "undressed" by Balanchine over the years they remained in the repertory. Both ballets premièred with specially designed costumes and décors, but *Apollo*'s costumes were greatly simplified, *The Four Temperaments*' abandoned in favor of black and white.

The dresses for *Serenade* (1935), Balanchine's first work in America, furnish a striking example of the choreographer's concern for bodily legibility and mobility. It is a "romantic" work performed to Tchaikovsky's Serenade in C for Strings, and the dancers' skirts resemble the long, full tulle skirts developed in the French romantic period to lend an ethereal quality to the dancing of that period's sylphs and wilis. In the romantic ballet, these skirts mask the movements of the leg and conceal the body's exertions, enveloping the lower extremities in a cloud of gauzy tulle.

The skirts that Barbara Karinska (with Balanchine) developed for *Serenade*, convey a similar otherworldliness, but Karinska's skirts differ from their romantic models in two important ways. First, they are not as full as the traditional skirts; they are lighter and more motile. In performance, the skirt "flies" to a much greater extent than those typically worn in the nineteenth century, in accordance with the quicker tempi and invigorated choreography of Balanchine's romantic reverie. They are also more revealing. The front of the skirt contains a white panel of tulle that shows the workings of the legs more clearly. Thus, even in a work with obvious historical allusions, with costumes dictated more or less by tradition, the Balanchinian priorities are apparent.

Balanchine's interest in exposing the dancing body is hardly prurient. Rather, his costumes reveal the material of his choreography. From the filmy skirts that masked the mechanics of the sylphide's legs, to the knee-length coat Pavl Gerdt donned as Désiré in *Sleeping Beauty*, the vertical strivings of the nineteenth-century's heroes and heroines were cloaked in the mystery of propriety. Balanchine's refusal to dissemble the body in traditional ballet costumes extends to a frank acknowledgment (and examination) of the dancing body's physicality, the revelation of the beauty inherent in the dance's academic technique. His decision to include visible bodily effort as an element of his choreography corresponds to Mandelshtam's incorporation of the logos, or conscious sense of the word: both involve the "inartistic," vernacular qualities of their media in the creation of art.

Unkind weight

Conventional attempts to hide the dancing body address the ballet's primary problem, the struggle to overcome gravity. Dance writers typically identify the quest of verticality as the ballet's cardinal rule.[5] But the human body's natural limitations place additional limits on its potential as a material for artistic composition. For Balanchine, the body's finite strength and flexibility presented other problems to overcome.

In the spirit of Mandelshtam's formulation of acmeism (an aesthetic which does not shrink from the "weight" of its materials, but enthusiastically exploits their potential (1987, 169)), Balanchine incorporates these perceived negative qualities in the choreography. In his discussion of Mandelshtam's "Notre Dame," Peter Steiner points out that "material cannot be disregarded, but only overcome; it must be reorganized and restructured with the skill of a Gothic builder" (1977, 252). This process of overcoming the material becomes a salient feature of Balanchine's art.

In *The Four Temperaments* (1946),[6] a ballet whose title suggests a consideration of physical qualities (as well as an allusion, like Mandelshtam's, to medieval culture), Balanchine carries out a programmatic examination of the dancing body's capabilities and limitations. In the same way that Apollo's first variation tests his own physical abilities (recalling a Mandelshtam poem that begins: "I've been given a body, what to do with it?" (1928, 11)), *The Four Temperaments* represents an examination of the body as material, and its potential in dance composition.

The Hindemith score begins with a statement of three themes. Four variations (temperaments) follow for various combinations of dancers. Already in the statement of the themes, the choreographer draws attention to the human body's inherent gravity, what Mandelshtam in "Notre Dame" had called "unkind weight" ("I too will someday make beauty from unkind weight" (ibid., 42)). At the end of a typical nineteenth-century pas de deux, the ballerina is borne off the stage – carried or escorted – by her cavalier. At the end of the first theme of *The Four Temperaments* the man grasps his partner under her arms with her legs and arms fully extended and rigid, feet barely touching the floor. He then carries – or seems to slide – her off the stage like some unwieldy piece of sculpture (Illustration 4).

In the second and third themes the choreographer varies the positioning of the woman's supported pirouette slightly to focus attention on the body's weight. Supported multiple turns are among the more spectacular effects of Petipa's choreography. Typically, the man stands behind the woman, "assisting" her multiple pirouette by spinning her on point. In *The Four Temperaments* the supported turns are performed slowly, with the women's legs slightly bent in plié. The bent leg and the slow revolution reveal both the force and strength the movement requires (Illustration 5).

The second and third themes explore the limits of the body's flexibility. In the third, the woman's leg is extended behind the body, grasped by her partner and stretched back and forth and from side to side. This motif repeats in the ballet's "Choleric" section, when four men manipulate the limbs of the soloist (Illustration 6). Like the woman in the ballet's first theme, the third-theme woman is also dragged along the stage, this time clinging to the man's torso. These moves – repeated, expanded, and transformed throughout the ballet – represent intensive examinations of the material of dance, its potential and limitations, and most importantly, its vulnerability to the force of gravity. That pull is demonstrated most explicitly in the work's "Melancholic" and "Phlegmatic" solos.

By the 1940s, when *The Four Temperaments* was created, the acknowledgment of gravity was a commonplace of modern dance. (Nijinsky's *Sacre* used gravity as a compositional element already in 1913.) But Balanchine's use of weight and exploration of the body represented something quite different. Balanchine refused to dissimulate, instead choosing to celebrate the very properties of his material that the classical ballet had traditionally concealed. In those moments of *The Four Temperaments* the means of academic dancing become as important as their end.

4 *The Four Temperaments.* Zippora Karz, Ben Huys.

6 *The Four Temperaments.* Diana White, Arch Higgins, Nilas Martins, Ben Huys, Jock Soto.

Mobile fetters

In *The Four Temperaments* Balanchine explores the body's constraints and limitations and the classical ballet's specific means of overcoming them. Other works examine these same issues, but add movement to the equation, focusing on a more specific, but related transformation: the overcoming of inertia, the body's shift from rest to motion – in essence, the transformation of the ordinary, earthbound human body to one seemingly free of its obligations to gravity, rigidity, and fatigue. The human bridges, chains, tunnels, and barriers in Balanchine's choreography – and the oppositions they imply – focus attention on this moment of transformation, when the body loses its familiar heaviness and becomes a dancing body, an aerial form to which centuries of training grant a degree of illusory lightness.

This type of examination typically assumes a slightly confrontational form in Balanchine's choreography, with one body blocking another's movement, or groups of dancers forming paths or barriers to direct or impede the course of others. In *Concerto Barocco*, set to Bach's Double Violin Concerto in D Minor, two female soloists dance passages that suggest (but do not mirror) the fugal counterpoint of the violins. Repeatedly, the two soloists appear to oppose each other, alternating quickly between movement and stasis, kinetic potential and corporeal constraint. At times, a soloist leaps across a conditional barrier formed by other dancers (Illustration 7). In the "Phlegmatic" section of *The Four Temperaments*, four dancers weave a complex web of arms and legs through which the soloist attempts to pass (Illustration 8).[7]

At these points in Balanchine's choreography, the body becomes part of a larger scheme, a unit in a three-dimensional construct. The animated structures – and their continual transformation, from body as obstacle to body in motion – are Mandelshtam's "mobile fetters of existence" (1987, 172), the ever-changing conditions of artistic composition that must constantly be overcome. This rapid manipulation of the material in Balanchine's choreography juxtaposes the body's motionless and mobile states in much the same way that Mandelshtam describes the material of "Notre Dame": the "heavy mass of stone" and the "light groin vault" are the same. In each case, the poet and the choreographer celebrate the duality of their materials, their ability to transform the commonplace and unlovely into things of beauty. They celebrate the transcendent powers of their arts.

7 *Concerto Barocco.* Merrill Ashley.

Hypnotizing space

The investigation of three-dimensional space (as a compositional element and as metaphor) represents yet another correspondence between the poetics of Balanchine and the acmeists. For Mandelshtam, three-dimensional space represented a void to be filled; construction – a means of conquering space and emptiness. Three-dimensional space represents the most basic condition of construction – a condition that must be as familiar to the architect as the material itself. Balanchine's interest in three-dimensional stage space is already evident in *Apollo*, his response to Nijinsky's "flat," anti-academic *Faune*. But in *Apollo*, Balanchine shows less interest in pictorial arrangement of groups within the proscenium than with the space itself: the way the body defines itself within that space, how groups of dancers can be used to define specific volumes of space, and how those volumes can interact in a dance.

Balanchine's treatment of stage space is as frank as his use of the body, essentially exposing it in the same way. There is no illusion of false perspective or recession, as in the Petipa ballet. Rather, Balanchine begins where Nijinsky left off in *Sacre*, the ballet that effectively invalidated the academy's traditional stagings. Balanchine does not disregard his public – the dances are still "shown" to an audience. But these dances no longer presume an "ideal" spectator – one who sits in the center of the theater's parterre or in its first ring. Many of Balanchine's works are best seen from the upper balconies of the theater, where the floor patterns and the resulting play of spatial volumes is more distinct. Balanchine's spatial organization is much more objective than that of Petipa in this regard, a nod to the ballet's origins in renaissance banquet halls, where dances were viewed from all sides, and the patterns described on the floor furnished the dance's chief interest.

One of the choreographer's more intriguing uses of stage space is demonstrated in the 1977 filming of *The Four Temperaments* for television broadcast. As with most of the Balanchine works filmed for the Dance in America television series in the 1970s, the space for dance is not clearly delineated, allowing the filming to take place from a variety of angles. In the first of the ballet's variations, "Melancholic," the dancer's solo is shot primarily from the front of the "stage." The male soloist is joined by two female dancers, then four more, whose entrance on-stage is comprised of a series of deliberate, high kicks. These four form a square at the back of the stage. The other dancers remain near the front of the stage, diagonally across from them.

125

In a particularly harrowing moment, the male soloist faces the four and charges into the square they describe. The camera records this on the diagonal, from behind the soloist, emphasizing the distance he travels, dramatically heightening this "gauntlet run." This simple shift of the camera angle emphasizes a process of identification inherent in Balanchine's choreography. Even without the technological advantage of shifting camera angles (i.e. in the theater) the sense of entrapment is palpable, particularly when the soloist attempts to free himself from the arms of the women surrounding him.

Balanchine was not the first ballet choreographer to show the moving body from a variety of vantage points. Petipa's choreography frequently shows the repeated movements of soloists from different angles.[8] But Balanchine exaggerates this technique. Like an architectural construct that can only be appreciated by moving through or walking around it, the structures formed in Balanchine's choreography (the bridges, tunnels, and barriers) grant a degree of audience participation, involving the spectator in the same way that the audience is drawn into the web of legs and arms that entraps the "Melancholic" soloist. This identification involves the spectator vicariously in the choreography to a much greater extent than in nineteenth- or even early twentieth-century choreography, whose ballets continued to be constructed as visual spectacles, "spectacle art" [*zrelishchnoe iskusstvo*].

The sense of entrapment from the webs woven in "Phlegmatic" section of *The Four Temperaments* or the cage constructed in "Melancholic" are palpable elements of Balanchine's choreography, choreographic "gestures" that involve the spectator of these works in the way that Gumilyov advocated in "The Life of Verse":

> By gesture in verse I mean such an arrangement of words, a selection of vowels and consonants, an acceleration and ritardando of rhythm, that the reader of the poem automatically assumes the pose of its hero, adopts his expression and movement, and thanks to suggestion of his own body, shares the experience of the poet himself, so that the thought expressed is already not a lie, but the truth.
>
> (1910, 8)

Jane Gary Harris discusses this "incipient" aspect of the acmeist canon "pertaining to the 'reader's' vicarious physiological and psychological experience" (1985, 4). Although few of Balanchine's ballets involve the spectator so blatantly as the "Melancholic" variation, the identification process in much of Balanchine's choreography is similar to the experience Gumilyov describes.

These "architectural" movement sequences – those which move the choreography "around" the spectator, so that choreographic structures are experienced architecturally rather than pictorially – underscore the inherent neutrality of Balanchine's stage space and the objectivity with which he approached it. The majority of Balanchine's ballets are staged on a flat stage in front of a blue cyclorama (like the "gray cloth" Bakst describes).[9] The actual volume of the stage remains absolute and fixed, but the absence of traditional perspective-stage trappings allows for its free manipulation. On-stage groupings of dancers define the stage space. Like acmeist verse, which emphasized the reader's immediate, palpable involvement in the poetry, Balanchine's spatial design involves the spectator in the space more directly. In this second phase of Russian modernism, the illusion of Petipa's stagings and the reliance on décor in Fokine's work (like the transcendent thrust of symbolist poetry) give way to more immediate, palpable pleasures afforded by twentieth-century art forms that find their nearest metaphors in the basic human activity of building.

Balanchine's re-apportionment of the stage space (the turn to human scale demonstrated so clearly in *Apollo*) has a genuine classical antecedent. The first-century architectural historian Vitruvius, whose writings provide the only contemporary treatise on classical architecture (see Hersey 1988, 2–3) addresses the human body in his discussion of the proportions of the classical temple: "No temple can have a reasonable form without symmetry and proportion if its parts do not exist in a certain relationship to one another, like the parts of a well-formed human being" (Von Naredi-Rainer 1992, 68). This article includes a number of Renaissance diagrams (recalling Leonardo's proportional drawing of the human body, after Vitruvius) that detail architecture's historical allegiances to the proportions of the body: the human body, arms outstretched, inscribed in the floor plan of a cathedral (the shape of the cross, after all); the body superimposed on a classical façade; a human head inscribed in a corinthian capital. Balanchine's use of stage space – that allowed the on-stage bodies to determine its perceived dimensions – represents an unwitting turn to this genuinely classical ideal: the conceptualization of "architectural" space on a human scale.

From stone to *Jewels*

In "The Paths of Classicism in Art," Bakst predicts a return to man and stone in the art of the future: "The painting of the future calls for a lapidary style. . . . The elements of recent painting are air, the sun, greenery. The elements of future art: man and stone" (1909, II, 61). Bakst wrote his essay at the time the future acmeists (who would soon dominate *Apollon*'s literature section) had begun writing and publishing their important early works. By 1909, Kuzmin's *Nets* (*Seti*) was well known, Akhmatova's verse was appearing in print, and Mandelshtam had begun *Stone* (*Kamen'*),[10] his first volume of poetry. The acmeists' regard for tangible, immediate human experience and the "lapidary" style of their well-crafted, comprehensible verse, anticipated Bakst's call.[11]

Balanchine's 1967 ballet *Jewels* represents the culmination of a series of works that, like the acmeists' early poetry, investigates the essential conditions of his craft. Described as the ballet's first full-length plotless work, the ballet is comprised of three distinct "acts." "Emeralds," the first, performed to incidental music of Gabriel Fauré, celebrates the evanescent beauty of the French romantic tradition, with long tulle skirts and demure choreography. "Rubies" is a brash affair, danced to Stravinsky's capriccio for piano and orchestra. "Diamonds" concludes the work. Set to the last three movements of Tchaikovsky's Third Symphony, the movement pays homage to the Petipa tradition, with drooping, nineteenth-century tutus for the corps and a brilliant polonaise as its finale.

Gems give the ballet its name and decorate the costumes, but the ballet's subject is the history of classical dancing. The individual qualities of the three precious stones correspond to the distinguishing features of the ballet's three main revivable dance styles: early nineteenth-century French, late nineteenth-century Russian, twentieth-century American. *Jewels* recapitulates another history as well: the work summarizes much of Balanchine's choreography, including works that represent stylistic precedents to the individual sections of *Jewels*. The ballet also refers to a series of works Balanchine choreographed to symphonies (and symphonically constructed works).

The idea for a ballet with a jewel theme had been with Balanchine for some time (even if a trip to the jeweler's inspired the work, as was widely reported). Balanchine spent six months in 1947 as guest ballet master of the Paris Opera, the home of the world's oldest dance academy. There he staged

Apollo, *Le Baiser de la fée*, and *Serenade* and choreographed a new work, *Le Palais de cristal*, to Georges Bizet's recently discovered Symphony No. 1 in C Major.[12] Richard Buckle mentions a scenario for the work that features "a Ruby Priestess, a Sapphire Spirit, an Emerald Spirit and a Crystal Spirit in a Palace of Diamonds" (1988, 165), but the ballet was produced without a plot. Instead, each of the symphony's four movements represented the qualities of a particular jewel. Leonor Fini supplied costumes in appropriate colors (red, blue, green, and white) and an architectural backdrop.[13] Balanchine staged the work for the Ballet Society the following year, retitling the work *Symphony in C*, and substituting black and white costumes for the colored ones used in Paris. (The small size of the American troupe required that dancers appear in more than one movement.)[14]

Though its relative brevity might not invite comparison, *Symphony in C* is Balanchine's answer to Petipa's grand ballet. Like most of Balanchine's works, the ballet is only as long as the concert music upon which it is based, and performed without special décor or costumes. But the size of the ballet's cast and its division into four distinct movements lend the work a distinctly "grand" variety and sweep.[15] Vadim Gaevsky likens the structure of *Symphony in C* to that of a pas classique: entrée, adagio, variation, coda (1931, 305). But the work's organization also recalls the formula of the Petipa *ballet à grand spectacle*: exposition, white act, and divertissement.

The allegro vivo movement that opens the work has the immediacy of an overture, it both "alerts" the audience and draws them quickly into the spectacle. The placement and ambience of the adagio that follows identify the movement as the work's *ballet blanc*, the apotheosis of the nineteenth-century ballet's dead heroine. Balanchine's ballerina is not dead, but dying; her repeated falls into the arms of her cavalier become the movement's leitmotif. As it ends, she falls in a long spiral, until, like Aurora, she lies in her partner's arms in a perfect fifth position, arms *en couronne*.

Balanchine choreographed a grand finale to the work's brisk fourth movement. After the exposition of the movement's musical and choreographic theme, the lead dancers are replaced on-stage by the personnel of the first, second, and third movements. All four groups assemble for the ballet's finale; they execute a series of relatively simple steps en masse in four columns headed by soloists, the ballerinas and their partners. The configuration updates the usual hierarchical assemblage that crowned the Petipa ballet, with its on-stage personnel grouped in semi-circles around the ballerina. Balanchine's finale blends the static hierarchical arrangement of the Petipa finale with the ordered infinity of his predecessor's vision scenes. The finale of *Symphony in C* is an inverted neoclassical façade with corps de ballet columns and a pediment of ballerinas (Illustration 9), an emblematic reference to the classical dance's orders, its symmetry, and the perfection of its form. Balanchine's crystal palace is an energized kingdom of shades.

Marina Konstantinova (1990) characterizes *Sleeping Beauty* as a grand Petersburg palace in her monograph on that ballet. In his discussion of the same work in *Divertissement*, Gaevsky speaks to the general role of palace architecture in Petipa's choreography:

> Most frequently, an architectural landscape furnished the backdrop for Petipa's ballets. The palace (classical as a rule, or perhaps baroque) became a nearly indispensable locale. In almost every ballet the décor bore a palace motif: the throne room, esplanade, colonnade, gallery, terrace, or some other ideal ensemble, in which one could easily recognize a Versailles-like facade, the fountains of Peterhof, or the parks of Tsarskoe Selo [the tsar's summer residence]. The world of Petipa was inseparable from the palaces drawn on his décors. This wasn't a court ballet, rather, it was a ballet *alongside* beautiful architecture. In Petipa's time, beautiful architecture was primarily the architecture of the court, as it once had been the architecture of the church.
>
> (1981, 93)

Balanchine's *Palais* returns to this nineteenth-century ideal, but his version of the grand ballet is no mere miniature. Rather, the ballet marks a decision to build the ballet/palace on a new foundation: the firm musical footing of the symphony.

Balanchine created a number of grandly scaled ballets that contrast the more theoretically ambitious modernist works that established his reputation as a ballet innovator. *Ballet Imperial* (1941) and *Theme and Variations* (1947) are tributes to imperial ballet style; they attain grandeur in purely classical terms, deploying masses onto the stage in exalted, nineteenth-century finales. In 1964, when the New York City Ballet first performed on the large stage in the New York State Theater, Balanchine restaged *Nutcracker* to fit the new space and revived *Ballet Imperial* for the first time with his own company. Several "grand" works followed: *Harlequinade* and *Don Quixote* in 1965, *Brahms–Schoenberg Quartet* in 1966, *Jewels* in 1967.

Brahms–Schoenberg Quartet (choreographed to Schoenberg's orchestration of Brahms' first piano quartet and danced before sets that depict gardens and architectural façades) was merely the latest in a series of "symphonic"

9 *Symphony in C.*

ballets, whose predecessors include the 1942 *Concierto de Mozart* (staged with an architectural décor by Pavl Tchelichev, Balanchine's frequent early collaborator) and *Gounod Symphony* (1958). When Charles Gounod's first symphony came to public attention ten years after *Palais de cristal*, Balanchine choreographed the work for his company. The Paris Opera staging of the ballet the following year bore the title *Symphonie*. The New York City Ballet production of *Gounod* is set in a French garden, in front of an iron and glass structure that recalls the original crystal palace.

Balanchine's "symphonic" ballets adapt the structure the choreographer used in *Symphony in C*. The symphony (or symphonized string quartet in the case of *Brahms–Schoenberg*) provided the choreographer a harmonious diversity that allowed for an examination of various dancing styles within a coherent, logically developed whole.[16] The correlation of the symphonic musical genre and architectural design in these works is significant: the symphony, a unified composition of contrasting segments, is the most "architectural" of musical forms, with its over-arching structure to which the individual movements accede. The idea of the ballet as superstructure, unified by repeated motifs and developed themes, is suggested both by the musical structures and the architectural drops that frame the majority of these works. Both the designs and the musical structures reveal the choreographer's continued interest in the investigation of the ballet's three-dimensional, architectural qualities and the material body's place within that scheme.

Jewels represents an extension of *Symphony in C*'s exploration of the material and substance of classical dance. Produced with only minimal scenery (typical of Balanchine works of this later period), the ballet makes no direct references to architecture, yet its links to the earlier "architectural" works are clear. The jewels in question, emeralds, rubies, and diamonds, are the same as those used in *Palais*.[17] In the same way that qualities such as color and cut distinguish gems, the phrasing and articulation of identical movements in *Jewels* differentiate the work's three separate styles of dancing.

Mandelshtam is said to have characterized acmeism as a "longing for world culture" [*toskva po mirovoy kul'ture*] (1977, 253). Balanchine's *Jewels*, a homage to the ballets of second empire Paris, late imperial Petersburg, and present-day New York, addresses that very issue. Referring at once to this history of ballet, to Balanchine's own œuvre, and to a specific series of his works that placed choreography on a plane with symphonic and architectural construction, the work's investigation of the distinctive qualities of balletic movement and style links *Jewels* to the choreographer's earlier explorations of material and space (*Apollo, The Four Temperaments*).

Like *Sleeping Beauty, Ruses d'amour, Pavillon d'Armide, Chopiniana*, and *Apollo, Jewels* is a balletic backward glance, a reminder of what had come before. Yet like *Sleeping Beauty* and *Apollo* (and unlike the last Petipa and the Fokine works), *Jewels* represents an advance, rather than a retreat, for the classical academy. Though Balanchine's New York City Ballet routinely offered evenings of plotless works, *Jewels* was the first of Balanchine's abstract ballets to take its place with the nineteenth-century's full-length productions. That precedent represented a watershed in both the production and reception of ballet in the twentieth century. The "plot" and subject of *Jewels* is the ballet academy; the enthusiastic response on the part of its audiences (Reynolds describes *Jewels* as a "box-office sensation" (1977, 247)) signaled the ultimate acceptance of dance over décor in twentieth-century ballet. Where *Ruses d'amour, Pavillon d'Armide*, and *Les Sylphides* had miniaturized older balletic genres, *Jewels* expanded upon the dance styles of the past, bringing them to the fore, making them the subject of the work.

Bakst predicted in 1909 that the nude figure and stone would be the elements of future art. Forgoing the psychological explorations that characterize the work of his Soviet and British contemporaries, Balanchine concentrated on the body and its potential in his choreography. That the qualities of precious stones would serve as the vehicle for two of his most important studies (*Symphony in C, Jewels*) seems only appropriate in this context. Mandelshtam's *Stone* (1913) is a first collection, full of promise – the practical expression of much early acmeist theory. Balanchine choreographed *Jewels* near the end of his career. It represents a summary of his work and contribution to the art of dance as it investigates the qualities of the ballet's main historical styles. *Jewels* is the highly polished analog of Mandelshtam's stone, a final acmeist homage to a tradition of Petersburg art.

APPENDIX

Unsigned reviews of performances

Sleeping Beauty

Peterburgskaya gazeta. 4 January 1890, 3.
Peterburgskaya gazeta. 16 January 1890, 3.
Peterburgsky listok. 5 January 1890.
Syn otechestva. 4 January 1890, 3.

Don Quixote (Gorsky)

Novoe vremya. 22 January 1902, 4.
Peterburgskaya gazeta. 1 September 1901.

Television broadcasts

Balanchine. 1984. PBS, Dance in America.
Choreography by George Balanchine I. 1977. PBS, Dance in America.
Stravinsky and Balanchine: Genius has a Birthday. 1982. PBS, Live from Lincoln Center.

Catalog

The Diaghilev–Lifar Library. 1975. Monaco: Sotheby Parke Bernet.

NOTES

1 Russian ballet in the late nineteenth century

1   The romantic movement in ballet dates from the production of Meyerbeer's *Robert le Diable* at the Paris Opera in 1831. (Taglioni starred in this production.) In the opera's ballet, dead nuns rise from their graves and waltz. This spectral corps de ballet initiated the romantic ballet's fascination with depictions of the spirit world and ethereal ballerinas.

2   Petipa shared choreographic duties with Antoine Titus until 1850, with Jules Perrot from 1848 to 1859, and with Arthur Saint-Léon from 1859 until 1869.

3   Slonimsky lists 76 ballets in his catalog of Petipa's ballets for the imperial theaters (1971, 377–388). This figure is arbitrary, since it is impossible to establish the authorship of some of the works. Many of the ballets attributed to Petipa were restagings of other choreographers' ballets that were partially or entirely re-choreographed by Petipa. Slonimsky includes *Nutcracker* (1892) (a ballet whose choreography is generally attributed to Petipa's assistant, Lev Ivanov) and

Romance of the Rosebud (a ballet never produced) in his catalog of Petipa productions.

4 Lev Ivanov choreographed the second act of *Swan Lake*.

5 Each has four acts in five to eight scenes.

6 Beaumont's text is actually a free (uncredited) adaptation of a portion of Valerian Svetlov's "Mysli o sovremennom balete" [Thoughts on Contemporary Ballet] published in *Sovremenny balet* [*The Contemporary Ballet*] (1911, 15–56) and in French translation in 1912.

7 *Corsaire* was staged for the ballet of the Paris Opera in 1856 by Joseph Mazilier, six years before Petipa's earliest version. Three ballets based on Cervantes' *Don Quixote* were produced between 1750 and 1850 in Vienna, Paris, and Berlin. The libretto of *Bayadère* is derived from the same source as that of *Sacountala*, a ballet produced by Marius Petipa's brother Lucien in Paris in 1858 (Krasovskaya 1963, 265–266).

8 Théophile Gautier derived the libretto of *Giselle* from a Heinrich Heine version of the Slavic folk legend of the *vili* (wilis). In the ballet, Giselle is a peasant girl who goes mad and dies when she learns that her suitor, Albrecht, is an aristocrat already affianced to a noblewoman. Consistent with Slavic folk legends of betrothed girls who die before their marriages, Giselle becomes a wili and joins her sister spirits in the forest, where they entrap men and force them to dance until they die. In the ballet's second act Albrecht visits Giselle's grave and falls prey to the wilis, but Giselle intervenes to save his life.

9 Edgar Allen Poe maintained that "the death . . . of a beautiful woman is, unquestionably, the most poetic topic in the world" (87–88). Bram Dijkstra discusses the prevalence of "Ophelias" and other depictions of dead women in mid-century painting in *Idols of Perversity* (25–63).

10 The ballet was often revived and remained in repertory ballet until 1928 (Krasovskaya 1963, 240–241).

11 *Daughter of the Pharaoh* is unique in this regard. The ballet's "white act," a fantasy scene within a dream sequence, is also unusual in that Aspichia – not the male protagonist – has the vision.

12 Ekaterina Vazem, the Petersburg ballerina of the 1860s–1880s, recalls the scenic effects employed in the Bolshoi Theater, St Petersburg's main ballet theater until 1885:

> It was ideally suited for ballet performances. It is true that the stage was not as wide as that of the Maryinsky Theater, but it was much deeper – there were seven wings. This was especially conducive to the performance's special effects, since it allowed for a broad use of perspective.

When, in *Corsaire*, the ship moves from the back of the stage to the front, or in *Bayadère*, when the row of shades looms in the cloudy distance, the effect was literally enchanting.

(1937, 49)

13 The 1890–1891 edition of the *Ezhegodnik imperatorskikh teatrov* [*The Yearbook of the Imperial Theaters*] lists eight *dekoratory* with ten assistants in the Petersburg theaters. In 1890, the Maryinsky theater claimed the services of one machinist with two assistants, and three electricians. The ballet had its own costumiers and wigmaker (*Ezhegodnik* 1890–1891, 111–113).

14 Petipa's composers included Cesare Pugni from the 1850s to the early 1870s, Ludwig Minkus in the 1870s and 1880s, and Riccardo Drigo in the final years of Petipa's career.

15 The choreographic notations of 24 imperial ballets, including *Sleeping Beauty*, are part of the Sergejev Collection of the Harvard Theatre Collection. The notations are based on a system devised by Vladimir Stepanov and revised by Aleksandr Gorsky and used in the imperial theaters between 1892 and 1913 (see Wiley 1976).

16 Saint-Léon's ballerinas were also supported in their pas de deux, but the memoirs of Vazem and other dancers of the period suggest that Petipa utilized point technique to a much greater extent than had his predecessors.

17 Petipa used 64 shades for the ballet's original production on the deep stage of St Petersburg's Bolshoi Theater in 1877. When the ballet moved to the shallower stage of the Maryinsky, their number was reduced to 32 (Gaevsky 1981, 70).

18 The experimentation and innovation on Russian dramatic stages, for example, was stimulated in part by a touring drama troupe from Germany. The Duke of Meiningen's drama troupe introduced a modern conception of direction and naturalistic staging when the company toured Russia in 1885 and 1890, furnishing a model for Konstantin Stanislavsky's Moscow Art Theater. Vsevolod Meyerhold, a Stanislavsky protégé, left the experimental wing of the Art Theater to direct several productions for Vera Komissarzhevskaya's private theater before he joined the imperial theaters, where he staged a number of landmark productions.

19 Krasovskaya blames the predominance of the Wagnerian opera in Western Europe for this decline, since Wagner's opera excluded ballet as an intrinsically dramatic element of the production.

The Russian ballet, according to Krasovskaya, remained healthy because it continued to reflect the "life of the human spirit": "It was this interest in man that the Russian theater took from the romantic ballet, then featured in the grand scheme, prejudicially leaving behind the living, dynamic national tradition of its art" (1963, 278).

Krasovskaya's argument is curious, since Petipa's choreography has generally outlived his librettos. She argues that even in the visual splendor of *Daughter of the Pharaoh*, the "drama of human passions and fortunes" predominates (ibid., 279). This is a forced reading, since revivals of the Petipa ballets have, for the most part, done away with the mimed narrative sequences Krasovskaya champions and preserved the choreography. *La Bayadère* continues to be performed in an abbreviated version, even though the fourth act, now omitted, is central to the ballet's "passions and fortunes." Likewise, the *jardin animé* scene and pas de deux of *Le Corsaire* are frequently staged, independent of the ballet's jumbled narrative, and the grand pas of *Paquita* has outlasted the rest of the ballet. Petipa's final full-length work, *Raymonda* (1898), has a hopelessly convoluted plot, but extraordinary choreography. The quality and quantity of the choreography in *Raymonda* evidence Petipa's interest in dancing, rather than narrative, late in his career.

20 Lyubov Blok views the late nineteenth-century obsession with point technique as the culmination of a process begun in the 1860s, when foreign dancers such as Henriette D'Or were alreading adapting pre-existing choreography to flaunt their technical capabilities. Blok takes an unusual position regarding the Italian ballerinas and their technical prowess:

> The urge towards virtuosity was an organic step in the development of the Russian school; a reaction against naturalism on the one hand, and a hedonistic attitude toward dance on the other. The Italians came just in time to show how it could be done and what could be achieved.
>
> (1987, 305)

2 *Sleeping Beauty*: *Ballet-féerie* as *Gesamtkunstwerk*

1 Petipa was not ignorant of "good" music, nor was this his first experience with it. He had staged approximately 40 opera ballets in

the imperial theaters by this time (Slonimsky 1971, 386–388), including works by Gluck, Verdi, Wagner, Bizet, Delibes, and Glinka. His inclusion of music from Delibes' ballet *La Source* (1866) in the 1868 restaging of *Le Corsaire* demonstrates Petipa's awareness of the music of his European contemporaries, as does his staging of *A Midsummer Night's Dream* (1876) to Mendelssohn's score.

2   The collaboration anticipated Petipa's work with Aleksandr Glazunov in the Hermitage Theater when Vsevolozhsky became director there in 1899.

3   Benois borrows Wagner's term – variously translated as "total art work" or "synthesis of the arts" – to describe the successful blending of the individual elements that comprised *Sleeping Beauty* (dance, music, décor, drama). The term came into general use in Russia to describe the ascendancy of the director/producer as the nineteenth-century theater's star system began to erode. Benois' use of the term represents a popularized notion of Wagner's theory that cast theater innovators such as Stanislavsky and Diaghilev – and others who sought to assimilate the elements of their theaters into coherent wholes – as Wagnerians.

4   Petipa's role in the genesis of the libretto should not be overlooked. His outline of the ballet (for Tchaikovsky) (Slonimsky 1971, 129–136) served as a detailed choreographer's plan of the entire production with indications of the future ballet's choreography, staging, and the type of music Petipa requested of his composer.

5   The ballet celebrates the writer's other works in the final act, populated by characters from Perrault's tales. The costumes and décor of that act, in Louis XIV style, will be discussed later in the chapter. It should be remembered, however, that Louis XIV and Perrault were contemporaries, and even though the reference to the Versailles court is the more significant, Perrault's fables play an important role in Vsevolozhsky's recreation of the golden age of French absolutist culture.

6   The ballet's prolog, chronologically antecedent to the ballet's main action, functions formally as an appendage to the ballet structure described here.

7   Chronologically, and in its implications for Russian art, the decision to revive the traditions of French court ballet in *Sleeping Beauty* corresponds to the travels undertaken by several prominent writers of the period. Dmitry Merezhskovsky traveled to Italy and Greece in

1891; Mikhail Kuzmin traveled to Alexandria and Italy a few years later. Their travels (like those of other writers to similarly "ancient" destinations) provided important source material and inspiration for the various revivals in Russian culture nearer the turn of the century.

8   Lyubov Blok stresses Johansson's knowledge of the French tradition, and asserts that Johansson – rather than Petipa – was the true heir to the French dancing tradition, having studied with August Bournonville, also a pupil of Auguste Vestris (Blok 1987, 309). This assertion is provocative, as many historians insist that Johansson choreographed many of the male variations in Petipa's ballets, or that Petipa "stole" from him. Although Petipa also studied with Vestris, and thus provides a more direct link to the old French tradition, Blok virtually dismisses Petipa's "happenstance development as a dancer in his nomadic family of provincial dancers" (ibid., 309).

9   Matvei Shishkov designed this scene.

10   In fact, what passed for a museum-like re-creation of period style on the Petersburg ballet stage in 1890 was still a far cry from the naturalistic theatrical productions staged by Stanislavsky and his followers in the next decades in Russia. Photographs of the first production of *Sleeping Beauty* reveal an ever-present tension in ballet costuming and design: a group photo shows Carlotta Brianza as Aurora amidst pages and fairies. All are in reasonable approximations of eighteenth-century costume except Brianza, who wears point shoes and tights, a dress with a contemporary corseted bodice over a tutu, and an 1890s hairstyle. The problem of the conventional ballet costume was mitigated somewhat by designing two types of costumes: one "authentic," for processionals, another for actual dancing. None the less, Petipa's daughter, Maria, in a "walking" role as the Lilac Fairy, wore heeled shoes and a long dress; "her Lilac Fairy resembled a grand dame calling at the palace after a fashionable reception" (Smakov 1989, 20).

Even in the early years of the twentieth century, the period of high naturalism on the Russian stage, the ballet theater could not abandon the contrivances of three centuries of convention. Mikhail Fokine and Aleksandr Gorsky, both aware of the developments on Russian dramatic stages in the first decades of the twentieth century, made valiant attempts to bring the ballet in line with the tenets of the "new" theater in Russia, but the ballet proved a less than ideal medium of naturalistic expression.

11   Korovyakov (1890) notes the inappropriateness of the dance's meter: the farandole is traditionally a dance in duple, not triple time.

12   The reviewer for *Peterburgskaya gazeta* found the final entrée particularly puzzling: ". . . in conclusion, a Roman sarabande, a Persian (?) sarabande, an Indian (??) sarabande, and American (???) sarabande, and even a Turkish (????) sarabande." And recapitulating: "The ballet concludes with five sarabandes. There are Turks and Americans, and Persians, and even Romans! . . . Whatever you wish! . . ." (4 January 1890).

13   The following day, the same paper objected to the ballet's mixture of French and Russian names in the ballet's program, dismissing the disturbing trend as "foreigner-worship" (4 January 1890).

14   This problem concerned Tchaikovsky as he composed *Swan Lake* (1877). John Warrack discusses Tchaikovsky's attempt to fuse narrative and pure dance sequences cohesively:

> A basic tonality could be identified with the central dramatic idea, and the substance of the action related by key to this. With it firmly established as the centre of a key-complex, the placing of an entire act in an unrelated key could become an expressive symbol of the drama taking an unexpected or threatening course; while within these long-range key-patterns, the introduction of divertissements in unrelated keys . . . would serve to indicate both musically and dramatically that they were incidental to the main progress of the drama.
>
> (1979, 12)

Roland Wiley discusses the thematic links in the score of *Sleeping Beauty* in *Tchaikovsky's Ballets*, (1985, 113–120).

15   Petersburg's balletomanes have traditionally borne the brunt of much unflattering press, but their arguments against *Sleeping Beauty* reveal the serious side of their connoisseurship. Skalkovsky and the critic for *Peterburgsky listok* argue for the primacy of dance in the ballet spectacle and the expressive quality of pure dance. Both of these arguments would figure prominently in the debates surrounding the "new" ballet and Diaghilev's Ballets Russes in the next decade. The lack of dramatic/narrative content of Western twentieth-century ballet and its emphasis of abstract or "pure" dance would continue to distinguish Western contemporary choreography from that of Soviet ballet choreographers.

16   Karsavina (who recalls a newspaper account putting the cost of the ballet at 40,000 rubles) suggests that the opulence of the production

was in part a stage trick: "Our chief costumier, Kaffi, at times found some ingenious economical devices; for instance, the ostrich feathers in the *Sleeping Beauty* were all made of wool. They looked rich and even more theatrical than the real ones" (1981, 106). Others put the total cost of the production at 80,000 rubles (Smakov 1989, 21).

17   Certainly, the royal presence was strongly felt in the ballet world. Anatole Chujoy estimates that St Petersburg's nineteen courts and their retainers could themselves fill all the city's theaters (1948, 49). Tchaikovsky's brief diary account of the gala dress rehearsal of *Sleeping Beauty* records little more than the composer's pique at Alexander III's polite dismissal of the ballet ("Very nice") (1923, 149).

18   Slonimsky, who characterizes Vsevolozhsky as an experienced courtier and a political reactionary ("experienced courtier," "highly reactionary") (1956, 167), offers a Soviet perspective:

The "Francomania" characteristic of the 1890s formed the rapprochement of tsarism with the French ruling classes and found in the person of Vsevolozhsky one of its most hopeful advocates. Allying himself to his ruling class antipathy to the realistic and democratic tendencies of Russian art, holding the dramatic theater in contempt . . . cultivating in every way possible insignificant French comedy – the favorite entertainment of the tsar's family, Vsevolozhsky was the chief propagandist of retrograde foreign fashion in ballet. His "French mythological" tastes, as Rimsky-Korsakov characterized them, brought about no small disaster to theater taste, and to the ballet – in part:

(ibid., 168)

19   Benois corroborates: "In his Catalbutte, Stukolkin impersonated the very type of the absurdly zealous, conceited and servile courtier. There was no exaggeration or malice, but good-natured humour, behind which one felt the typical smile of Ivan Alexandrovitch [Vsevolozhsky] himself – a great but good-natured joker"(1941, 129).

20   *Peterburgskaya gazeta* judged the work "the complete downfall of the choreographic art" (4 January 1890).

21   A three-year renovation of the theater was completed in 1898 (Taranovskaya 1988, 44).

22   Petipa choreographed only one ballet in Vsevolozhsky's absence, *Magic Mirror* (1903). That ballet was generally judged a failure, and withdrawn after its second performance.

23   Period authenticity extended to the costumes as well. The *Rossiya* reviewer complained: "It would be hard to imagine something less

suited to particulars of the artist's talent [Legnani], considering the virtuosity of her technique, than to see her in a long dress, dancing a passe-pied or gavotte – very strange indeed!!" (25 January 1900).

24   The obsession with authenticity led indirectly to Sergei Volkonsky's resignation as Director of Imperial Theaters in 1901 when Matilda Kshesinskaya refused to perform in the paniers Camargo's costume required. (Kshesinskaya maintains the costume was a copy of a dress Catherine II wore at a ball honoring Joseph II (1961, 81).)

25   Petipa's 1898 ballet *Raymonda* represents an important step in the latter process. Its cumbersome plot has occasioned simplifications and revisions of the story line whenever the ballet has been restaged, but the work remains compelling as an abstract work, with a varied, seemingly endless string of pas and variations. Balanchine turned to the music from *Raymonda* (and to some of Petipa's choreography as well) to make four new ballets of his own.

26   Alexandre Benois, Walter Nouvel, Konstantin Somov, and Diaghilev's cousin, Dmitri Filosofov, comprised the original circle. Léon Bakst, Charles Birlé, Alfred Nourok, and Eugene Lanceray were among those later affiliated with the group.

3 Ballet Ruse: The Dying Swan

1   Fokine claims to have choreographed the work in 1905 for Anna Pavlova, although no record of this performance exists. Vera Krasovskaya discovered an affiche announcing the work's 1907 performance in Soviet archives (Money 1982, 71). As Fokine is known to have altered the dates of some of his early ballets in his memoirs, most scholars give 1907 as the date of the work's première. The questions regarding Fokine's chronologies will be discussed later in this chapter.

2   Plisetskaya even performed the work at a gala benefiting the Martha Graham company, an ironic inclusion, since Graham's relationship with Fokine was adversarial at best.

3   This is not to imply that a work's survival in the repertory assures its quality or contribution, or that lost works deserved their fates. But works that disappear do not play the same role in the evolution of the art form as those that are maintained in the repertory, to be seen by

future generations of choreographers and dance-goers.

4   In Moscow, the force of Gorsky's innovations was also grinding to a halt; the choreographer's efforts to revitalize the ballet hinged increasingly on complex narratives.

5   The Wanderers [*peredvizhniki*], a group of Russian visual artists that seceded from the state-supported academy of art in 1863, provide the earliest and most obvious example of this trend.

6   Blok addresses this issue candidly: "How, then, was this Fokine-ism reflected in the ballet school? Unfavorably, it must be said frankly" (1987, 331). Blok goes on to discuss the technical weaknesses of the dancers Fokine trained:

> From 1908 to 1918 the school failed to produce even one strong, well-trained dancer, although there were outstanding talents among the students: Lyukom, Spesivtseva. But they would be forced to finish their studies later, privately, when the wave of Fokinism subsided and they would confront the difficulties of the classical repertory face to face.
>
> (ibid., 331)

She then discusses the technical shortcomings of Fokine's most brilliant interpreters: Pavlova and Karsavina (ibid., 332–333).

7   The imperial theaters were themselves somewhat leaderless in those years. Vsevolozhsky's successor, Sergei Volkonsky, was an enlightened man sympathetic to new trends in art. His published works on dance suggest his potential to lead the imperial ballet into the modern era much as Vsevolozhsky had in the 1880s and 1890s, but that potential was never realized. Volkonsky was forced to resign in 1902, the result of a dispute regarding a costume worn by the ballerina Matilda Kshesinskaya, whose protectors included the tsar. Vladimir Telyakovsky, formerly a colonel in the cavalry, assumed the post from 1902 until 1917.

8   Kalbouss goes on to describe Nietzsche's influence on the works of Minsky, Bely, Merezhskovsky, Balmont, Annensky, Ivanov, and Sologub.

9   The Moscow Art Theater (MKhAT), founded in 1898, became famous for its naturalistic productions and the so-called "method" of acting Stanislavsky developed there, although the theater's most important contribution to Russian theater was its abolition of the star system. The new focus on the play's direction and the importance of the production as an entity resulted from the de-emphasis of a play's main performers. In this regard, the Art Theater responded to some

of the same problems of nineteenth-century theater production that *Sleeping Beauty* addressed some years earlier. Although *Sleeping Beauty* could hardly be considered "naturalistic," it too represented an important step in a Wagnerian direction. Stanislavsky's productions were authenticized to a degree neither possible nor desirable on the ballet stage, but like the Petipa–Vsevolozhsky work, Stanislavsky's productions paved the way for the sweeping innovations of the next decades on both the ballet and the dramatic stages.

10   Levinson also discussed the use of bare feet (where sandals were used in ancient Greek dance) as a conceit of bodily freedom, suggesting that Isadora would have preferred to perform nude (43–44). Ironically, her anachronistic use of nineteenth-century music to accompany "Greek" dances raised fewer critical hackles. The controversy surrounding Isadora's musical accompaniment (drawn primarily from the late romantic repertory) centered around the appropriateness of "serious" music for dance.

11   At the turn of the century, the term "*dekadenstvo*" (decadence) encompassed a multitude of improprieties, often of a sexual nature.

12   The meaning of this term is unclear.

13   The Aleksandrinsky Theater was the main dramatic theater in St Petersburg.

14   Russian architecture adopted similar terms to distinguish its new twentieth-century style: *style moderne* or *novy stil'* (new style) (Brumfield 1991, 47–48).

15   Stepanov's system was published in Paris in 1892 as *Alphabet des mouvements du corps humain*. The system was taught in the theater school in St Petersburg from 1893, but not published in Russia until Gorsky put out an abridged translation of Stepanov's work in 1899. The choreographic notations of late imperial ballets in the Sergejev Collection in the Harvard Theatre Collection are notated in this system (Wiley 1976).

16   Perrot staged *Esmeralda* in Russia in 1848. Petipa revived the work for Matilda Kshesinskaya in 1899. The ballerina added her own naturalistic touch, appearing on stage with a pet goat.

17   Beaumont also confuses Fokine's age, asserting that "the following extracts [of Fokine's notes] will make clear the wealth of perception and logic displayed by this young man of twenty-one" (1935, 23). Earlier, Beaumont gives Fokine's birth-date, correctly, as 1880, making Fokine twenty-four at the end of 1904.

18   In *Era of the Russian Ballet*, Natalia Roslavleva notes that no record of this submission exists in the imperial theater archives, but helpfully suggests that "it was probably considered unworthy of preservation in the files" (1966, 174).

19   The most recent (and exhaustively researched) work on the Diaghilev ballet, Lynn Garafola's *Diaghilev's Ballets Russes* (1989), accepts Fokine's dates.

20   Krasovskaya notes the libretto's similarities to A. K. Tolstoi's poem "Portrait" (1971, 196–197).

21   Blok continues: "Like many creators, Fokine obviously didn't understand his significance or his place in the history of dance. He underestimated the importance of *Sylphides* and over-rated his contradictory thoughts on classical dance, his superficial historicism, his naturalistic eroticism (*Schéhérazade*, *Egyptian Nights*)" (1987, 331).

22   Of course, these works' elaborate costumes and décor made them difficult to revive or maintain in the repertory. But their reliance on visual effects essentially excluded them from the body of works recognized (and revived) for the strength of their choreography.

23   Krasovskaya suggests that Fokine's *Eros* (1915) surpassed even the nineteenth-century ballet's great melodramas (*Bayadère*, *Esmeralda*) in its reliance on false sentiment and insincerity. What is more, he choreographed the ballet for Matilda Kshesinskaya, the "old" ballet's leading exponent (1971, 64).

4 Crisis in the academy: The death of the maiden

1   A number of useful essays and articles discuss the design and movement of Nijinsky's *Faune*. Charles S. Mayer's article "The Influence of Leon Bakst on Choreography" (1977) describes the genesis of *Faune* and the choreographer's debt to his visual designer. Lynn Garafola's description of *Faune*'s movement idiom in Diaghilev's *Ballets Russes* (1989, 57) is pithy and evocative.

2   Later Meyerhold productions continued to experiment with new methods of staging: Wagner's *Tristan and Isolde*, staged for the imperial theater in 1909, utilized a number of stage planes, his productions of Molière's *Don Juan* and Gluck's *Orpheus and Eurydice* (in

1910 and 1911) divided the stage into two distinct planes.

3   Millicent Hodson (1986–1987, 12) discusses the ritual implications of
     Roerich's designs.

4   The critic for *Peterburgskaya gazeta*, who translates the French names of
     Sleeping Beauty's cast list into Russian in his review, refers to Carabosse
     as *Gorbun'ya*, "the hunchback," (4 January 1890).

5 Two Apollos

1   Like many members of the Mir iskusstva group, *Apollon*'s founder,
     Sergei Makovsky, was a dilettante in the best sense of the word. He
     involved himself in poetry as well as visual art, and edited the art
     journals *Starye gody* [*The Bygone Years*] and *Russkie ikoni* [*Russian Icons*]
     before founding *Apollon*.

2   Bakst, Benois, Bilibin, Dobuzhinsky, Somov, and Diaghilev appeared
     on the masthead.

3   This trend was not limited to literature. In 1909, Bakst lamented his
     peers' fixation with the art of the past: "The contemporary
     generation knows the history of art only too well" (II, 60).

     In 1915, the reviewer of André Levinson's book on eighteenth-
     century dance, "An Unpublished Manuscript of Noverre," declared:
     "A new renaissance has occurred – a renaissance of the eighteenth
     century" (Slonimskaya 1915, 33). The review sparked a debate that
     continued in subsequent numbers of *Apollon*. That a review of a book
     on eighteenth-century dance would prompt a public discussion in an
     important journal suggests both the pervasiveness of the eighteenth
     century's renaissance, and the appeal of "classical" art, however
     broadly that term was understood in 1915.

4   This "rediscovery" of St Petersburg and its neoclassical architecture
     has important implications for the renaissance of the Russian ballet
     academy. Founded in 1703 as Russia's "Western" capital, St
     Petersburg remained Russia's conduit of Western art and culture. The
     imperial ballet was established there in 1738, and the fates of the city
     and its ballet remained inextricably linked. Their respective establish-
     ments in the eighteenth century and "fall" in the early period of
     Soviet power (the removal of the capital to Moscow in the Soviet
     period marked the end of the Petersburg ballet's hegemony) are not

coincidental. Both were symbols and products of Russian imperial power, which had conceived and maintained them.

5   Several groups of articles stand out from the *Ezhegodnik*'s plethora of performers' biographies and reminiscences. Seven different essays paid tribute to Glinka, the "father" of Russian music. Most articles on contemporary opera dealt in some way with Wagner ("Wagner, *Walküre*, and Wagnerism," "Serov: Was he a Meyerbeerist, a Wagnerian, or an Independent Composer?").

6   Skalkovsky covers a wide range of theatrical activity: state and private theaters, opera, operetta, provincial theaters, reform in the imperial theaters, and foreign troupes. Other chapters are purely subjective: "On the Right to Applaud, Call out Performers, and Move About in the Theater," "On Morality On-stage and Behind the Scenes."

7   Garafola cites Kenneth Silver's *Espirit de Corps: The Great War and French Art 1914–1925*. Like Garafola, Silver views the art of this period as a "retreat, expressed in a return to figurative styles and nationalist themes, as a response to the reactionary ideology promulgated as part of the war effort" (Garafola 1989, 116). In *Russian Art of the Avant Garde*, John Bowlt discusses Benois' "search for a cohesive style in the face of his 'spiritually tormented, hysterical time' . . . his aesthetic devotion to bygone cultures" (1988, 3). Bowlt's quote from Benois' conclusion to *The History of Russian Painting* (1902) suggests that while socio-political unrest might have played a role in the rise of twentieth-century classicism, Parisian art of the 1910s did not set the precedent.

8   Boris Kochno, the ballet's librettist, originally planned to present the work as an eighteenth-century Russian mythological ballet performed by serf artists (Buckle 1979, 431).

9   In a 1978 essay, Arlene Croce named only four Ballets Russes works that had survived "with the heat of inspiration still in them": Fokine's *Les Sylphides*, Nijinsky's *Faune*, Nijinska's *Les Noces*, and Balanchine's *Apollo* (Croce 1982, 106). Balanchine's *Prodigal Son* should be added to that list as well.

10 Balanchine's father, the composer Meliton Balanchivadze, studied composition at the conservatory with Rimsky-Korsakov. Meliton's brother, Vassily, studied at the Academy of Arts under Ilya Repin and Konstantin Makovsky, the father of Sergei Makovsky, the founder of *Apollon*. George Balanchine's sister became a painter, his brother, a composer (Slonimsky 1975–1976, 1).

11 The synopsis of the ballet which followed the opening credits of the

1982 PBS *Live from Lincoln Center* broadcast of *Apollo* (see Appendix, p. 135) reads as follows:

Entranced by music and song, the young god Apollo flexes his new-found body. Three muses dance for his delight – Calliope represents poetry; Polyhymnia – mime; and Terpsichore – the rhythms of dance. All are beautiful, but it is Terpsichore who captures his heart. At the command of Zeus, Apollo and the muses reluctantly return to the heights of Mount Olympus.

12   *Apollo* was subject to numerous revisions, most having to do with the ballet's beginning and end. The scenario described outlines the work's most basic plot. Revisions to the ballet will be discussed later.

13   To Vazem's dismay, the apple in the earlier ballet was diplomatically halved, "as benefit etiquette dictated" (1937, 156).

14   Petipa might also have known Jules Perrot's *Le Jugement de Paris*, given in London in 1846. That work featured three goddesses, three graces, Paris, Mercury, Cupid, Hymen, and nymphs. A lithograph of the main divertissement from the work, the "Pas des Déesses" is part of the iconography of romantic ballet (see Beaumont, 1941, facing page 255).

15   Alexandra Danilova staged *Les Sylphides* as *Chopiniana* for the New York City Ballet in 1972. That staging – danced by Peter Martins, a noted Apollo – used piano accompaniment (rather than the usual orchestrations of Chopin) and short white tunics for the women. The ambiguous pedagogical exchange in *Apollo* also recalls *Sleeping Beauty*. Wiley suggests that the fairies also benefit from their encounter with Aurora: "Petipa . . . unified some of the variations . . . with *enchaînements*, which required the dancers to face the cradle, thereby suggesting not just the giving of a blessing but also the receiving of some intangible gift – beauty or enchantment – from the child" (1985, 171–172).

16   *Giselle*, *La Sylphide*, *Nathalie ou la laitière suisse*, *La Gitana*, *Paquita*, *Daughter of the Pharaoh*, *La Bayadère*, *La Esmeralda*, *Sleeping Beauty*, and *Raymonda*, to name but a fraction. Mazilier's *Le Corsaire* and Perrot's *Faust* are notable exceptions.

17   Both *Apollo* and *Prodigal Son* (1929) were choreographed to showcase the questionable talents of Serge Lifar, then the *beau gosse* of the Ballets Russes and Diaghilev's favorite.

18   The iconography of Russian ballet from the middle of the nineteenth century until the Diaghilev period is rich with depictions (and often

conflations) of Apollo and *le roi soleil*. Apollo is the hero of *Dve zvezdy*, the Petipa court spectacle. He appears in the apotheosis of *Sleeping Beauty* dressed as Louis XIV. The viscount in *Le Pavillon d'Armide* imitates Louis' dress and hairstyle.

Apollo's links to the French court ballet are suggested as well in Stravinsky's conspicuous absence from the ballet's Washington, DC première. Arlene Croce writes that the composer expected the festival would generate more attention from the White House than it actually did (1982, 109).

19 Balanchine's revisions of *Apollo* are discussed in *Choreography by George Balanchine: A Catalogue of Works*, 1984, 86–87. Balanchine revised the ballet's beginning and ending several times. The ballet originally began with Apollo's birth and ended with the four dancers posed on a staircase at the back of the stage, representing the ascent to Parnassus. Balanchine omitted the birth scene in 1978 and re-choreographed the ending in 1979. Unless otherwise noted, all discussions of the ballet's choreography refer to Balanchine's final, 1979 version of the ballet. The birth scene that used to begin the ballet provided a kind of mimed prelude to the ballet, somewhat incongruous to the dancing that followed. In "Staging Balanchine's Ballets: A Symposium," Nancy Reynolds discusses Balanchine's eventual omission of the prologue:

> We should be aware that it was originally devised at least partly for commercial reasons. Kochno and Stravinsky could earn higher royalties from a ballet having two scenes or movements rather than just one. . . . The music for it actually duplicates later parts of the ballet and has no intrinsic reason for being there.
>
> (Dunleavy *et al.* 1983, 91)

20 The sunburst that concludes *Apollo* is only the last of a series of visual puns and allusions in the ballet: the muses' unusual *port de bras* evokes the sun's lunar trajectory; the troika they form in the coda is Apollo's chariot. These seemingly simplistic visual metaphors have a more basic purpose: they draw the audience's attention to the dancers' bodies. In this extreme example of medium as message, the audience must read movement – and its iconic allusions – rather than pantomimed narrative to arrive at the ballet's "meaning."

21 Balanchine's work represents a corrective to Nijinsky's, not an outright rejection. As Balanchine revived and revised *Apollo* over the next five decades, the work's increasing reliance on movement to convey

its succint narrative recalled the achievement of *Faune*. Without the mimed narrative prolog that began the ballet, movement alone conveys the action of *Apollo*.

6 Bodies and buildings

1   Although Mandelshtam's admiration for Gothic architecture appears anachronistic at a time when Petersburg architects were developing a new neoclassical style, Mandelshtam's eclecticism corresponds to Gumilyov's expanded notion of the "classic," discussed in the previous chapter.

2

> Avant-garde artists such as Stravinsky felt a sincere need for a return to classical standards, both during the war and after, when the full extent of the damage could be assessed. . . . The classical revival of the 1920s was born partly out of constructive hope for the future, partly out of nostalgia for what had seemed most secure in the past.
>
> (Johnson, 1985, 50)

3   Suritz also mentions artists such as Isadora Duncan, who danced in St Petersburg in 1922 and 1924. Alexandra Danilova recalls that she and Balanchine did see Duncan. Isadora's dancing made a favorable impression on Danilova, but Balanchine thought Isadora, by then in her forties, "a big pig" (Danilova 1989).

4   A poem Balanchine sent to Suzanne Farrell, the muse of his final decades, in 1963 furnishes further evidence of Balanchine's continued interest in and awareness of Russian poetry. As quoted in her 1990 autobiography, the poem, which begins "I can't forget this blessed vision," is a translation of the first three stanzas of Pushkin's "To . . ." [*Ya ponmyu chudnoe mgnoven'e*] (11–12) (Scholl 1991).

   Bart Cook, a New York City Ballet dancer, told the author in conversation (17 November 1988, New York City) that when he (Cook) had begun to choreograph, Balanchine told him that one must bear the metrics of poetry in mind when choreographing. Balanchine then began to recite Russian poetry.

5   Akim Volynsky's "The Vertical: The Fundamental Principle of Classic Dance" and Lincoln Kirstein's "Classic Ballet: Aria of the Aerial" (both in Copeland and Cohen 1983), for example.

6   The work was originally produced with costumes and décor by the surrealist artist Kurt Seligmann. From the first performances, Balanchine surreptitiously lopped off parts of the extraordinarily elaborate costumes. In staging the work for his New York City Ballet in 1951, Balanchine eliminated the décor and dressed his dancers in practice clothes.

7   A more refined statement of this movement motif is seen in the second movement of *Symphony in C*. As the ballerina balances on point in arabesque, soloists run between her and her partner. The ballerina's precarious pose heightens the juxtaposition of movement and perilous stasis.

8   In one of the variations of Petipa's *Paquita*, for example, the soloist performs a series of turns that describe a large half-circle covering the stage, from stage right to stage left. As the dancer repeats the movement from one side of the stage to the other, she shows the same movement, beginning to end, from all angles.

9

In order to emphasize that the spectator is not being treated to a "painterly" dancer against the background of an antique landscape, but rather a combination of distinct poses, the entire backdrop is impossibly simplified. It doesn't exist, the body stands out like a statue in a museum, against gray cloth.

(Bakst 1909, I, 60)

10   The title of Mandelshtam's first collection of poems alludes to a poem by the nineteenth-century metaphysical poet Fyodor Tyutchev. In the poem *"Problème,"* Tyutchev wonders whether a stone that lies in a ravine has rolled down the mountain of its own accord, or was prompted by some other will. In "The Morning of Acmeism" Mandelshtam declares that the acmeists will raise Tyutchev's stone and make it the cornerstone of their "building" (1987, 169).

11   Mandelshtam's "I've been given a body – but what to do with it" (1928, 11), the anthropomorphic stone cathedral of "Notre Dame" (ibid., 42).

12   The title of the work is somewhat cynical in the Russian context. Dostoevsky's underground man railed against the Crystal Palace (the emblem of the 1851 London exhibition of the same name) as a symbol of the ultimate triumph of moribund determinism and his century's blind positivism. Yet Balanchine presented the work in a real nineteenth-century palace – Charles Garnier's magnificent Opéra – without a hint of irony.

13 Photos in the library of the Opéra show dancers in front of a slightly surreal baroque façade, trimmed with menacing three-dimensional spikes. The backdrop and the costume designs (with antler-like head-pieces and vein-covered tutus) recall the work of Pavl Tchelichev, a Balanchine collaborator, who dabbled in rather gruesome organic art in this period.

14 The ballet grew with the New York City Ballet, so that by 1968 the work was performed by a full complement of 52 dancers (*Choreography by George Balanchine* 1984, 178).

15 Balanchine made an American version of *Symphony in C* in 1954, when he choreographed *Western Symphony*, a comic ballet, to an arrangement of traditional cowboy songs. The work mirrors the structure of *Symphony in C* down to its second-movement love duet and its fast-paced finale.

16 Ballets such as *Stars and Stripes* (1958), *Who Cares?* (1970), *Union Jack* (1976), and *Vienna Waltzes* (1977) use arrangements of music of one composer or of one epoch to similar ends.

17 Melissa Hayden, a ballerina who danced for Balanchine in the 1960s, maintains that Balanchine had intended to choreograph a "sapphires" movement as well (Tracy 1983, 117). In her autobiography, Suzanne Farrell speculates that Balanchine found no "blue" music to use for the ballet (1990, 160).

Earlier precedents also exist. The third act of *Sleeping Beauty* featured a pas de quatre for gold, silver, sapphire, and diamond fairies. That pas de quatre referred in turn to the eighteenth century's allegorical ballets, a tradition Petipa revived in works such as *Les Saisons* (1900).

BIBLIOGRAPHY

Anawalt, Sasha. 1987. "Joffrey's *Sacre* Reviewed." *Ballet Review* 15.2: 72–74.

Antimonov, S. I. 1971. Quoted in Krasovskaya, V. *Russky baletny teatr nachala XX veka.* [*Russian Ballet Theater at the Beginning of the Twentieth Century*]. Leningrad, 434.

Armstrong, Leslie, and Roger Morgan. 1984. *Space for Dance.* Washington, DC: Publishing Center for Cultural Resources.

Auslender, Sergei. 1909. "Tancy v 'Knyaze Igore.'" ["The Dances in 'Prince Igor'"]. *Apollon* 1: 29–30.

Bakst, Lev. 1909. "Puti klassicizma v iskusstve." ["The Paths of Classicism in Art"]. *Apollon* I. 2: 63–78; II. 3: 46–61.

——. 1921. "Tchaikowsky aux Ballets Russes." *Comoedia* 15 (19 October): 1.

Balanchine, George. 1982. "The Dance Elements in Stravinsky's Music." *Ballet Review* 10.2: 14–18.

——. 1985. Quoted in Volkov, Solomon. *Balanchine's Tchaikovsky.* Translated by Antonina W. Bouis. New York: Simon & Schuster.

Balanchine, George, and Francis Mason. 1977. *Balanchine's Complete Stories of the Great Ballets.* New York: Doubleday.

Beaumont, Cyril W. 1935. *Michel Fokine and His Ballets.* London: C. W. Beaumont.

——. 1941. *Complete Book of Ballets.* Garden City, New York: Garden City Publishing Co.

Belyaev, Yuri. 1971. Quoted in Krasovskaya, V. *Russky baletny teatr nachala XX veka.* [*Russian Ballet Theater at the Beginning of the Twentieth Century*]. Leningrad.

Benois, Alexandre. 1909. "I. A. Vsevolozhskij." ["I. A. Vsevolozhsky"]. *Rech'*, 1 November, 2–3.

—. 1910. "Balet v Aleksandrinke." ["A Ballet at the Aleksan-drinka"]. *Rech'*, 19 November, 3.

—. 1941. *Reminiscences of the Russian Ballet.* Translated by Mary Britnieva. London: Putnam.

—. 1971. Quoted in Krasovskaya, V. *Russky baletny teatr nachala XX veka.* [*Russian Ballet Theater at the Beginning of the Twentieth Century*]. Leningrad.

—. 1977. "Chem mogla by byt' Akademiya khudozhestv v nastoyashchee vremya." ["What an Art Academy Could be in the Present"], 95. Quoted in Kennedy, Janet. *The "Mir iskusstva" Group and Russian Art (1898–1912).* New York: Garland, 47–48.

—. 1980. *Moi vospominaniya* [My Reminiscences]. 2 volumes. Moscow.

Blok, L. D. 1987. *Klassichesky tanec: istoriya i sovremennost'* [*Classical Dance: History and the Present*]. Moscow.

Borisova, E. A., A. I. Venediktov, and T. P. Kazhdan. 1980. "Arkhitektura i arkhitekturnaya zhizn'" ["Architecture and Architectural Life"]. In *Russkaya khudozhestvennaya kul'tura.* [*Russian Artistic Culture*]. vol. 4, 1908–1917. Moscow. 297–364.

Boretsskoi, D. 1899. "Opera i balet pri I. A. Vsevolozhskom." ["Opera and Ballet under I. A. Vsevolozhsky"]. *Novoe vremya*, 9 August, 2.

Bowlt, John E., ed. and trans. 1988. *Russian Art of the Avant Garde: Theory and Criticism.* New York: Thames & Hudson.

Bristol, Evelyn. 1986. "Blok between Nietzsche and Soloviev." In *Nietzsche in Russia.* Edited by Bernice Glatzer Rosenthal. Princeton, NJ: Princeton University Press. 149–159.

Bryusov, Valery. 1902. "Nenuzhnaya pravda." ["Unnecessary Truth"]. *Mir iskusstva* 7.1-6: 67–74.

—. 1908. "Realizm i uslovnost' na scene." ["Realism and Convention on the Stage"]. In *Teatr: Kniga o novom teatre* [*Theater: A Book about the New Theater*]. St Petersburg.

Brumfield, William Craft. 1991. *The Origins of Modernism in Russian Architecture.* Berkeley, CA: University of California Press.

Buckle, Richard. 1979. *Diaghilev.* New York: Atheneum.

—. 1988. *George Balanchine, Ballet Master.* New York: Random House.

Choreography by George Balanchine: A Catalogue of Works. 1984. New York: Viking.

Chujoy, Anatole. 1948. "Russian Balletomania." *Dance Index* 7.3: 41–71.

Cohen, Marshall. 1983. "Primitivism, Modernism, and Dance Theory." In *What is Dance?* Edited by Roger Copeland and Marshall Cohen. New York: Oxford University Press.

Copeland, Roger and Marshall Cohen, eds. 1983. *What is Dance?* New York: Oxford University Press.

Cott, Jonathan. 1983. "Balanchine: Music and Dance." *Ballet Review* 11.3: 76–80.

Croce, Arlene. 1982. *Going to the Dance.* New York: Knopf.

Danilova, Alexandra. 1986. *Choura: The Memoirs of Alexandra Danilova.* New York: Knopf.

—. 1989. Interview by author, 13 July, New York City. Tape recording.

Dijkstra, Bram. 1986. *Idols of Perversity: Fantasies of Feminine Evil in Fin-de-Siècle Culture.* New York: Oxford University Press.

Drewal, Margaret Thompson. 1985. "Constructionist Concepts in Balanchine's Choreography." *Ballet Review* 12.3: 42–47.

Dunleavy, Rosemary *et al.* 1983. "Staging Balanchine's Ballets: A Symposium." *Ballet Review* 11.3: 81–96.

Eksteins, Modris. 1989. *Rites of Spring: The Great War and the Birth of the Modern Age.* New York: Doubleday.

Etkind, Mark. 1989. *A. N. Benua i russkaya khudozhestvennaya kul'tura.* [*A. N. Benois and Russian Artistic Culture*]. Leningrad.

Ezhegodnik imperatorskikh teatrov. [*Yearbook of the Imperial Theaters*]. Various years, esp. 1890–1891, 1892–1915. St. Petersburg.

Farrell, Suzanne. 1990. *Holding On to the Air.* New York: Summit.

Fokine, M. 1971. "Noch' Terpsichory." ["The Night of Terpsichore"]. Interview by "Teatral." *Peterburgskaya gazeta*, 21 January 1908, 4. Quoted in Krasovskaya, V. *Russky baletny teatr nachala XX veka.* [*Russian Ballet Theater at the Beginning of the Twentieth Century*]. Leningrad, 223, 224.

—. 1981. *Protiv techeniya: vospominaniya baletmeistera.* [*Against the Current: The Memoirs of a Balletmaster*]. Edited by Y. Slonimsky. Leningrad.

Gaevsky, V. 1981. *Divertisment.* [*Divertissement*]. Moscow.

Garafola, Lynn. 1989. *Diaghilev's Ballets Russes.* New York: Oxford University Press.

Glebov, Igor. [Boris Asafiev]. 1929. *Kniga o Stravinskom.* [*A Book about Stravinsky*]. Leningrad.

Gnedich, P. P. 1929. *Kniga Zhizni*. [*The Book of a Life*]. Edited by V. F. Botsyanovsky. Leningrad.

Goldner, Nancy. 1973. *The Stravinsky Festival of the New York City Ballet*. New York: Eakins Press.

Gorsky, Aleksandr. 1902. Interview. *Peterburgskaya gazeta*, 20 January.

Green, Michael. 1973. "Mikhail Kuzmin and the Theater." *Russian Literature Triquarterly* 7: 243–266.

Gumilyov, N. 1910. "Zhizn' stikha." ["The Life of Verse"]. *Apollon* 7: 5–14.

——. 1914. *Kamen'* O. Mandel'shtama. [Review of Mandelshtam's *Kamen'*]. *Apollon* 1–2: 126–127.

Gvozdev, Aleksei. 1990. "Molodoi balet." ["The Young Ballet"]. *Zhizn' iskustva*, 27 May 1924, 4. Quoted in *Soviet Choreographers in the 1920s*. Edited by Sally Banes. Translated by Lynn Visson. Durham, NC: Duke University Press, 76. [Author's name spelled "Souritz."]

Harris, Dale. 1982. "Balanchine: Working with Stravinsky." *Ballet Review* 10.2: 19–24.

Harris, Jane Gary. 1985. "Acmeism. Handbook of Russian Literature." New Haven, CT: Yale University Press.

Hersey, George. 1988. *The Lost Meaning of Classical Architecture: Speculations on Ornament from Vitruvius to Venturi*. Cambridge, MA: MIT Press.

Hodson, Millicent. 1986–1987. "Nijinsky's Choreographic Method: Visual Sources from Roerich for *Le Sacre du Printemps*." *Dance Research Journal* 18.2: 12.

Hoover, Marjorie. 1985. "The Russian Theater." *Handbook of Russian Literature*. New Haven, CT: Yale University Press.

Horwitz, Dawn Lille. 1987. "*Sacre* at the Joffrey." *Ballet Review* 15.3: 67–69.

Ivanov, Vyacheslav. 1905. "Vagner i dionisovo deistvo." ["Wagner and the Dionysian Drama"]. *Vesy* 2.11: 13–16.

——. 1908. "Nicshe i Dionis'." ["Nietzsche and Dionysus"]. *Vesy* 5: 17–30.

Jaques-Dalcroze, Emile. 1921. *Rhythm, Music and Education*. Translated by Harold F. Rubenstein. London: Chatto & Windus.

Johnson, Robert. 1985. "White on White: The Classical Background of *Apollon Musagète*." *Ballet Review* 12.3: 48–54.

Kalbouss, George. 1976. "The Birth of Modern Russian Drama." In *Russian and Slavic Literature*, ed. Richard Freeborn, *et al.* Cambridge, MA: Slavica Publishers, 175–189.

——. 1986. "Echoes of Nietzsche in Sologub's Writings." In *Nietzsche in Russia*, ed. Bernice Glatzer Rosenthal, 181–194. Princeton, NJ: Princeton University Press.

Karsavina, Tamara. 1971. "Romantika i volshebstvo tanca." ["The Romance and Magic of Dance"]. In *Marius Petipa: materialy, vospominaniya, stat'i. [Marius Petipa: Materials, Reminiscences, Articles]*, ed. Yuri Slonimsky, 303–313. Leningrad.

——. 1981. *Theatre Street*. London: Heinemann, 1930; reprint, London: Dance Books Ltd (page references are to reprint edition).

Kennedy, Janet. 1977. *The "Mir iskusstva" Group and Russian Art (1898–1912)*. New York: Garland.

Khudekov, S. N. 1913–1918. *Istoriya tancev. [The History of Dances]*. 4 volumes. St Petersburg/Petrograd.

Kirstein, Lincoln. 1947. "Balanchine Musagète." *Theatre Arts* November, 37–41.

——. 1979. *Thirty Years of the New York City Ballet*. London: A. & C. Black.

——. 1984. *Four Centuries of Ballet: Fifty Masterpieces*. New York: Dover.

Konstantinova, M. 1990. *Spyashchaya krasavica [Sleeping Beauty]*. Moscow.

Koptyaev, A. 1900. "A. K. Glazunov, kak baletny kompozitor." ["A. K. Glazunov as a Ballet Composer"]. *Ezhegodnik imperatorskikh teatrov*. Supplement 1, 49–59.

Korovyakov, D. D. ["N."] 1890. "Novy balet." ["The New Ballet"] *Novosti i birzhevaya gazeta*, 5 January, 3.

Kostylev, N. 1910. "Nash balet v Parizhe." ["Our Ballet in Paris"]. *Apollon* 9: 25–29.

Kranchenko, N. 1902. "Novye dekoracii «Don Kikhota»." ["The New Décor of *Don Quixote*"]. *Peterburgskaya gazeta*, 29 January, 3.

Krasovskaya, V. 1963. *Russky baletny teatr vtoroi poloviny 19-go veka. [Russian Ballet Theater of the Second Half of the Nineteenth Century]*. Leningrad.

——. 1971. *Russky baletny teatr nachala XX veka. [Russian Ballet Theater at the Beginning of the Twentieth Century]*. Leningrad.

Krivenko, V. S. 1909. "I. A. Vsevolozhsky." *Novoe vremya*, 30 October, 3.

Kshesinskaya, Matilda [spelled Mathilde Kschessinska]. 1961. *Dancing in Petersburg*. Translated by Arnold Haskell. New York: Doubleday.

Kuzmin, M. 1910. "O prekrasnoi yasnosti." ["On Beautiful Clarity"]. *Apollon* 4: 5–10.

Levin, David Michael. 1983. "Balanchine's Formalism." In *What is Dance?* Edited by Roger Copeland and Marshall Cohen. New York: Oxford University Press.

Levinson, André. 1911a. "O novom balete." ["On the New Ballet"]. *Apollon* I. 8: 30–49. II. 9: 16–29.

——. 1911b. "O moskovskom balete." ["On the Moscow Ballet"]. *Apollon* 10: 160.

—. 1913a. *O starom i novom balete.* [*On the Old and New Ballet*]. *Ezhegodnik imperatorskikh teatrov.* 1: 1–20.

—. 1913b. "Russky balet v Parizhe." ["The Russian Ballet in Paris"]. *Rech'*, 3 June, 2.

—. 1913–1914. "Balety Nizhinskogo (*Svyashennaya vesna – Igry*)." ["Nijin-sky's Ballets (*Le Sacre du printemps, Jeux*)"]. *Masky* 4: 32–39.

—. 1921. "Une dernière étape des «Ballets Russes»: *La Belle au bois dormant.*" *La Revue Musicale* 1 December: 131–135.

—. 1982. *Ballet Old and New.* Translated by Susan Cook Summer. New York: Dance Horizons.

Lifar, Serge. n.d. *A History of Russian Ballet from its Origins to the Present Day.* Translated by Arnold Haskell. New York: Roy.

Lukomsky, G. 1914. "Neo-klasicizm v arkhitekture Peterburga." ["Neoclas-sicism in Petersburg Architecture"]. *Apollon* 5: 5–20.

Lunacharsky, A., et. al. 1908. *Teatr. Kniga o novom teatre.* [*Theater: The Book of the New Theater*]. St Petersburg.

Maeterlinck, M. 1900. "Sovremennaya drama." ["Contemporary Drama"]. Translated by V. M. *Mir iskusstva* 4: 227–232.

Makovsky, Sergei. 1909. "Vstuplenie." ["Introduction"]. *Apollon* 1: 3–4.

Mandel'shtam, Osip. 1928. *Stikhotvorenie.* [*Poems*]. Leningrad.

—. 1977. Quoted in Steiner, Peter. "Poem as Manifesto: Mandel'stam's 'Notre Dame.'" *Russian Literature.* 3: 253.

—. 1987. *Slovo i kul'tura.* [*The Word and Culture*]. Moscow.

Mayer, Charles S. 1977. "The Influence of Leon Bakst on Choreography." *Dance Chronicle* 1.1: 127–142.

Mickiewicz, Denis. 1975. "*Apollo* and Modernist Poetics." In *The Silver Age of Russian Culture*, ed. Carl and Ellendea Proffer, 360–395. Ann Arbor: Ardis.

Minsky, N. 1912. "Sensacionny balet (Pis'mo iz Parizha)." ["A Startling Ballet (a Letter from Paris)"]. *Utro rossii*, 24 May, 2.

Money, Keith. 1982. *Anna Pavlova.* New York: Knopf.

Naredi-Rainer, Paul Von 1992. ". . . Like the Parts of a Well-formed Human Being." *Daidalos*, 15 September: 64–71.

Paglia, Camille. 1990. *Sexual Personae: Art and Decadence from Nefertiti to Emily Dickinson.* New Haven, CT: Yale University Press.

Petipa, M. 1896. Interview by V. P. *Peterburgskaya gazeta*, 2 December, 2. Quoted in Slonimsky, Yuri. *P. I. Chaikovsky i baletny teatr ego vremeni.* [*P. I. Tchaikovsky and the Ballet Theater of his Time*]. Moscow, 123.

—. 1940. Quoted in Bakhrushin, Y. A. "Balety Chaikovskogo i ikh scenicheskaya istoriya." ["Tchaikovsky's Ballets and their Stage History"]. In *Chaikovsky i teatr: stat'i i materily.* [*Tchaikovsky and the Theater: Articles and Materials*]. Edited by A. I. Shaverdyan. Moscow, 107.

—. 1987. "Programma baleta *Spyashchaya krasavica*." ["The Program of the Ballet *Sleeping Beauty*]." In P. I. Tchaikovsky, *Spyashchaya krasavica* [*Sleeping Beauty*], piano redaction by A. Ziloti. Edited by A. N. Dmitriev. Moscow: 274–84.

Petrov, O. A. 1989. "*Spyashchaya krasavica* Mariusa Petipa – dve tochki zreniya." ["Marius Petipa's *Sleeping Beauty* – Two Points of View"]. In *Sergey Dyagilev i khudozhestvennaya kul'tura XIX–XX vv.* [*Sergei Diaghilev and the Artistic Culture of the Nineteenth and Twentieth Centuries*]. Perm, 30–36.

Pierpont, Claudia Roth. 1990. "Maenads." *The New Yorker*, 20 August, 82–91.

Pleshcheev, Aleksandr. 1896. *Nash balet (1674–1896).* [*Our Ballet*]. St Petersburg.

Poe, Edgar Allen. 1985. Quoted in Hoffman, Daniel. *Poe, Poe, Poe.* New York: Doubleday, 1972; reprint 1985, New York: Vintage (page references are to reprint edition).

Pogozhev, V. P. n.d. *Vospominaniya.* [*Reminiscences*]. St Petersburg.

Ponomarev, E. 1898–1900. "I. A. Vsevolozhsky." ["I. A. Vsevolozhsky"]. *Ezhegodnik imperatorskikh teatrov.* [*Yearbook of the Imperial Theaters*]. St Petersburg, 25–32.

Prokofyev, V. 1900. "Malenkaya khronika: Bal khudozhnikov." ["The Little Chronicle: The Artists' Ball"]. *Novoe vremya*, 15 February, 3.

Reyna, Ferdinando. 1965. *A Concise History of Ballet.* Translated by Pat Wardroper. New York: Grosset & Dunlap.

Reynolds, Nancy. 1977. *Repertory in Review: Forty Years of the New York City Ballet.* New York: Dial.

Rivière, Jacques. 1983. "Le Sacre du Printemps." In *What is Dance?* Edited by Copeland, Roger and Marshall Cohen, 115–123. New York: Oxford University Press.

Roerich, Nikolai. 1971. Quoted in Krasovskaya, V. *Russky baletny teatr nachala XX veka.* [*Russian Ballet Theater at the Beginning of the [Twentieth Century]*]. Leningrad, 429.

Rosenthal, Bernice Glatzer, ed. 1986. *Nietzsche in Russia.* Princeton, NJ: Princeton University Press.

Roslavleva, Natalia. 1966. *Era of the Russian Ballet.* London.

Rudnitssky, K. L. 1969. *Rezhisser Meierkhol'd.* [*Meyerhold the Director*]. Moscow.

Rykwert, Joseph. 1992. "Körper und Bauwerk/Body and Building." *Daidalos*, 15 September: 100–109.

Saltykov-Shchedrin, N. 1935. *Polnoe sobranie sochinenii*. [*Collected Works*]. Leningrad.

Scholl, Tim. 1991. "Balanchine's 'Blessed Vision.'" *Ballet Review* 19.2: 28–29.

Skalkovsky, K. 1890. "Teatr i muzyka." ["Theater and Music"] *Novoe vremya*, 5 January, 3.

—. 1899. *V Teatral'nom mire*. [*In the Theater World*]. St Petersburg.

Slonimskaya, Yu. 1915. "Neizdannaya rukopis' Noverra." ["An Unpublished Manuscript of Noverre"]. *Apollon* 1: 33–45.

Slonimsky, Yuri. 1956. *P. I. Chaikovsky i baletny teatr ego vremeni*. [*P. I. Tchaikovsky and the Ballet Theater of his Time*]. Moscow.

—, ed. 1971. *Marius Petipa: materialy, vospominaniya, stat'i*. [*Marius Petipa: Materials, Reminiscences, Articles*]. Leningrad.

—. 1975–1976. "Balanchine: The Early Years." Translated by John Andrews. *Ballet Review* 5.2: 1–64.

Smakov, Gennady. 1989. "Marius Petipa and the Creation of *The Sleeping Beauty*." In *100 Years of Russian Ballet, 1830–1930*. Edited by Nancy Van Norman Baer. 17–22. New York: Nakhamkin.

Stark, E. A. [Zigfrid]. 1911. "Renessans baleta." ["The Ballet Renaissance"]. *Ezhegodnik imperatorskikh teatrov*. St Petersburg, 102–122.

—. 1915. "Novye balety Fokina." ["Fokine's New Ballets"]. *Apollon* 10: 64–67.

Steiner, Peter. 1977. "Poem as Manifesto: Mandel'stam's 'Notre Dame.'" *Russian Literature*. 3: 239–256.

Stravinsky, Igor. 1927. "Avertissement." *The Dominant*, 1.2: 13–14.

—. 1962. *An Autobiography*. New York: Simon & Schuster. 1936; reprint, New York: Norton (page references are to reprint edition).

—. 1971. Quoted in Krasovskaya, V. *Russky baletny teatr nachala XX veka*. [*Russian Ballet Theater at the Beginning of the Twentieth Century*]. Leningrad, 429.

Stravinsky, Vera, and Robert Craft. 1979. *Stravinsky in Pictures and Documents*. New York: Simon & Schuster.

Summer, Susan Cook. 1982. Introduction to *Ballet Old and New*, by André Levinson. Translated by Susan Cook Summer. New York: Dance Horizons.

Suritz, Elizabeth. 1977. "Baletnoe iskusstvo." ["The Art of Ballet"]. In *Russkaya khudozhestvennaya kul'tura*. [*Russian Artistic Culture*]. vol. 3, 1908–1917. Moscow, 341–364.

——. 1990a. *Soviet Choreographers in the 1920s*. Edited by Sally Banes. Translated by Lynn Visson. Durham, NC: Duke University Press [author's name spelled "Souritz"].

——. 1990b. "The Young Balanchine in Russia." *Ballet Review* 18.2: 66–71.

Svetlov, Valerian. 1909. "Mysli o sovremennom balete." ["Thoughts on Contemporary Ballet"]. *Ezhegodnik imperatorskikh teatrov*. St Petersburg. Supplements 6–7, 27–48.

——. 1911. *Sovremenny balet*. [*The Contemporary Ballet*]. St Petersburg.

Taranovskaya, M. Z. 1988. *Arkhitektura teatrov Leningrada*. [*The Architecture of Leningrad's Theaters*]. Leningrad.

Taruskin, Richard. 1982. "From *Firebird* to *The Rite*: Folk Elements in Stravinksy's Scores." *Ballet Review* 10.2: 72–87.

Tchaikovsky, Modest. 1989. Quoted in Smakov, Gennady. "Marius Petipa and the Creation of *The Sleeping Beauty*." In *100 Years of Russian Ballet, 1830–1930*. Edited by Nancy Van Norman Baer. 17–22. New York: Nakhamkin.

Tchaikovsky, P. I. 1923. *Dnevniki* [*Diaries*]. Edited by Ip. I. Tchaikovsky. Moscow.

——. 1974. *Polnoe sobranie sochinenii. Literaturnye proizvedeniya i perepiska*. [*Collected Works. Literary Works and Correspondence*]. Edited by A. N. Aleksandrov, *et al.* vol. 1. Moscow.

Telyakovsky, V. A. 1965. *Vospominaniya*. [*Reminiscences*]. Moscow.

Tolstoy, Lev. 1898. *Chto takoe iskusstvo?* [*What is Art?*]. London.

Tracy, Robert. 1983. *Balanchine's Ballerinas, Conversations with the Muses*. New York: Linden Press/Simon & Schuster.

Turgendkhold, Y. 1910a. "Russky balet v Parizhe." ["The Russian Ballet in Paris"]. *Apollon* 8: 69–71.

——. 1910b. "Russky sezon v Parizhe." ["The Russian Season in Paris"]. *Apollon* 10: 5–23.

Valts, K. F. 1928. *Shest'desyat pyat' let v teatre*. [*Sixty-five Years in the Theater*]. Leningrad.

Vashkevich, Nikolai. 1905. "Dionisovo deistvo sovremennosti. Eskiz o sliyanii iskusstva." ["The Contemporary Dionysian Drama. A Sketch on the Synthesis of Art"]. *Skorpion* 14–15.

——. 1908. *Istoriya tancev vsex vremen i narodov*. [*The History of Dances of All Times and Peoples*]. St Petersburg.

Vazem, Ekaterina. 1937. *Zapiski baleriny Sankt-peterburgskogo Bol'shogo teatra 1867–1884*. [*The Memoirs of a Ballerina of the St. Petersburg Bolshoi Theater*]. Leningrad.

Vitruvius. 1914. *Ten Books on Architecture*. Translated by Morris Hicky Morgan. Cambridge, MA: Harvard University Press.

—. 1992. Quoted in Von Naredi-Rainer, Paul. ". . . Like the Parts of a Well-formed Human Being." *Daidalos*, 15 September: 68, 69.

Volkonsky, Sergei. 1913. "Russky balet v Parizhe." ["The Russian Ballet in Paris"]. *Apollon* 70–74.

Volkov, Solomon. 1985. *Balanchine's Tchaikovsky*. Translated by Antonina W. Bouis. New York: Simon & Schuster.

Vsevolozhsky, I. A. 1956. Quoted in Slonimsky, Yuri. *P. I. Chaikovsky i baletny teatr ego vremeni*. [*P. I. Tchaikovsky and the Ballet Theater of his Time*]. Moscow, 169.

Warrack, John. 1979. *Tchaikovsky Ballet Music*. Seattle: University of Washington Press.

Wiley, Roland John. 1976. "Dances from Russia: An Introduction to the Sergejev Collection." *Harvard Library Bulletin* 24: 96–112.

—. 1985. *Tchaikovsky's Ballets*. Oxford: Oxford University Press.

Yakovlev, M. A. 1924. *Baletmeister Marius Petipa*. [*The Balletmaster Marius Petipa*]. Leningrad.

Znosko-Borovsky, E. A. 1925. *Russky teatr nachala XX veka*. [*Russian Theater in the Beginning of the Twentieth Century*]. Prague: Plamya.

INDEX